OPPOSING VIEWPOINTS® SERIES

Robotic Technology

Other Books of Related Interest:

Opposing Viewpoints Series

Medical Technology

Nanotechnology

At Issue Series

Drones

Technology and the Cloud

"Congress shall make no law . . . abridging the freedom of speech, or of the press."

First Amendment to the US Constitution

The basic foundation of our democracy is the First Amendment guarantee of freedom of expression. The Opposing Viewpoints series is dedicated to the concept of this basic freedom and the idea that it is more important to practice it than to enshrine it.

OPPOSING
VIEWPOINTS®
SERIES

Robotic Technology

Louise Gerdes, Book Editor

GREENHAVEN PRESS
A part of Gale, Cengage Learning

GALE
CENGAGE Learning·

Farmington Hills, Mich • San Francisco • New York • Waterville, Maine
Meriden, Conn • Mason, Ohio • Chicago

GALE
CENGAGE Learning®

Elizabeth Des Chenes, *Director, Content Strategy*
Cynthia Sanner, *Publisher*
Douglas Dentino, *Manager, New Product*

© 2014 Greenhaven Press, a part of Gale, Cengage Learning

WCN: 01-100-101

Gale and Greenhaven Press are registered trademarks used herein under license.

For more information, contact:
Greenhaven Press
27500 Drake Rd.
Farmington Hills, MI 48331-3535
Or you can visit our Internet site at gale.cengage.com

For product information and technology assistance, contact us at

Gale Customer Support, 1-800-877-4253
For permission to use material from this text or product, submit all requests online at
www.cengage.com/permissions

Further permissions questions can be emailed to permissionrequest@cengage.com

Articles in Greenhaven Press anthologies are often edited for length to meet page require-ments. In addition, original titles of these works are changed to clearly present the main thesis and to explicitly indicate the author's opinion. Every effort is made to ensure that Greenhaven Press accurately reflects the original intent of the authors. Every effort has been made to trace the owners of copyrighted material.

Cover image copyright © Chris Rogers/Corbis.

LIBRARY OF CONGRESS CATALOGING-IN-PUBLICATION DATA

Robotic technology / Louise Gerdes, book editor.
    p. cm -- (Opposing viewpoints)
    Summary: "Opposing Viewpoints: Robotic Technology: This title addresses vari-ous issues related to robotic technology, centered around the questions of Is Ro-botic Technology Beneficial?, What Role Should Robotic Technology Play in War?, and What Are the Ethical, Legal and Moral Considerations Surrounding Robotic Technology?"-- Provided by publisher.
    Includes bibliographical references and index.
    ISBN 978-0-7377-6338-6 (hardback) -- ISBN 978-0-7377-6339-3 (paperback)
    1. Robotics--Moral and ethical aspects--Juvenile literature. 2. Technology and state--Juvenile literature. I. Gerdes, Louise I., 1953-
    TJ211.2.R63 2013
    629.8'92--dc23
                                                            2013029732

Printed in the United States of America
1 2 3 4 5 6 7 18 17 16 15 14

Contents

Chapter 2: What Role Should Robotic Technology Play in War?

Chapter 3: What Ethical, Legal, and Moral Issues Relate to Robotic Technology?

Why Consider Opposing Viewpoints?

> *"The only way in which a human being can make some approach to knowing the whole of a subject is by hearing what can be said about it by persons of every variety of opinion and studying all modes in which it can be looked at by every character of mind. No wise man ever acquired his wisdom in any mode but this."*
>
> *John Stuart Mill*

In our media-intensive culture it is not difficult to find differing opinions. Thousands of newspapers and magazines and dozens of radio and television talk shows resound with differing points of view. The difficulty lies in deciding which opinion to agree with and which "experts" seem the most credible. The more inundated we become with differing opinions and claims, the more essential it is to hone critical reading and thinking skills to evaluate these ideas. Opposing Viewpoints books address this problem directly by presenting stimulating debates that can be used to enhance and teach these skills. The varied opinions contained in each book examine many different aspects of a single issue. While examining these conveniently edited opposing views, readers can develop critical thinking skills such as the ability to compare and contrast authors' credibility, facts, argumentation styles, use of persuasive techniques, and other stylistic tools. In short, the Opposing Viewpoints Series is an ideal way to attain the higher-level thinking and reading skills so essential in a culture of diverse and contradictory opinions.

In addition to providing a tool for critical thinking, Opposing Viewpoints books challenge readers to question their own strongly held opinions and assumptions. Most people form their opinions on the basis of upbringing, peer pressure, and personal, cultural, or professional bias. By reading carefully balanced opposing views, readers must directly confront new ideas as well as the opinions of those with whom they disagree. This is not to argue simplistically that everyone who reads opposing views will—or should—change his or her opinion. Instead, the series enhances readers' understanding of their own views by encouraging confrontation with opposing ideas. Careful examination of others' views can lead to the readers' understanding of the logical inconsistencies in their own opinions, perspective on why they hold an opinion, and the consideration of the possibility that their opinion requires further evaluation.

Evaluating Other Opinions

To ensure that this type of examination occurs, Opposing Viewpoints books present all types of opinions. Prominent spokespeople on different sides of each issue as well as well-known professionals from many disciplines challenge the reader. An additional goal of the series is to provide a forum for other, less known, or even unpopular viewpoints. The opinion of an ordinary person who has had to make the decision to cut off life support from a terminally ill relative, for example, may be just as valuable and provide just as much insight as a medical ethicist's professional opinion. The editors have two additional purposes in including these less known views. One, the editors encourage readers to respect others' opinions—even when not enhanced by professional credibility. It is only by reading or listening to and objectively evaluating others' ideas that one can determine whether they are worthy of consideration. Two, the inclusion of such viewpoints encourages the important critical thinking skill of objectively evaluating an author's credentials and bias. This evaluation will illuminate an author's reasons for taking a particular stance on an issue and will aid in readers' evaluation of the author's ideas.

It is our hope that these books will give readers a deeper understanding of the issues debated and an appreciation of the complexity of even seemingly simple issues when good and honest people disagree. This awareness is particularly important in a democratic society such as ours in which people enter into public debate to determine the common good. Those with whom one disagrees should not be regarded as enemies but rather as people whose views deserve careful examination and may shed light on one's own.

Thomas Jefferson once said that "difference of opinion leads to inquiry, and inquiry to truth." Jefferson, a broadly educated man, argued that "if a nation expects to be ignorant and free . . . it expects what never was and never will be." As individuals and as a nation, it is imperative that we consider the opinions of others and examine them with skill and discernment. The Opposing Viewpoints series is intended to help readers achieve this goal.

David L. Bender and Bruno Leone,
Founders

Introduction

"At bottom, robotics is about us. It is the discipline of emulating our lives, of wondering how we work."

—Rod Grupen,
computer science professor and
director of the Laboratory for
Perceptual Robotics at the University
of Massachusetts, Amherst

The controversies surrounding robotic technology are at times as complex as the technology itself and intimately connected to what it means to be human. From the perspective of the robotic engineer, a robot is a device that performs functions that a human might perform, and robotics is a branch of science that involves the design of robots and the computer systems that control them. For most robot-designing engineers and researchers, known as roboticists, the goal of robotic technology is to develop robots that will perform in a manner similar or superior to humans tasks that are dangerous, unpleasant, or too challenging for humans. For others, the goal is to replicate human behavior and intelligence as part of the quest to better understand the human mind.

For those who are not robotic technology engineers, the word *robot* often conjures images drawn from science fiction, in which the authors ask and attempt to answer geopolitical, moral, and social questions about human/robot interaction. In fact, the word *robot* was first used in the 1921 play *R.U.R. (Rossum's Universal Robots)*, by Czech writer Karel Čapek. The name comes from the Slavic word *robota*, which means "slave labor." Although the play's robots were organic, the word came to represent mechanical creations. Čapek's robots, while initially content to work for people, ultimately become dissatisfied with their slave status and destroy the human race. Indeed, the fear of a robot apocalypse is a common theme of robot science fiction to this day. At present, however, robots serve primarily practical functions. Most bear little resemblance to humans and with limited intelligence pose no real threat. The field of robotics is developing rapidly, however, and many roboticists aim to develop robots that interact more intimately with people. How best to address the challenges that this increasing interaction may pose is explored by both science fiction writers and robotic engineers alike, and while the robots of fiction bear little resemblance to the robots of reality, both perspectives inform the robotic technology debate.

From helpful human companions such as R2-D2 and C-3PO of the *Star Wars* movies to the agents of the robot apocalypse in the *Terminator* franchise, the robots of science fiction bear little similarity to the robots that work in factories, diffuse bombs in Iraq, or rove the surface of Mars. Nevertheless, the robots of science fiction inspire robotic technology. In fact, scientist, philosopher, and prolific science fiction author Isaac Asimov is credited with the first use of the word *robotics* to describe the science of robot engineering in the 1941 short story "Liar!" Asimov's fiction also influenced early robotics engineers. George Devol designed the first programmable robot, called UNIMATE, in 1954, and with Joseph Engelberger, who built the first prototype, formed the first company to manufacture robots. Indeed, Engelberger is often called the father of robotics, and he attributes his fascination with robots to reading Asimov's *I, Robot*, the collection of short stories in which "Liar!" appeared, as a teen.

Although Asimov is best known as a writer of science fiction, robotics engineers often cite his three laws of robotics in discussions of robot ethics. These laws first appeared in the short story "Runaround" (also in *I, Robot*) in 1942. The First Law is that a robot may not harm a human being or, through inaction, allow a human being to come to harm. The Second Law requires that a robot must obey orders given it by human beings, except where such orders would conflict with the First Law. The Third Law necessitates that a robot must protect its own existence as long as such protection does not conflict with the First or Second Law. While these laws appear to reflect the guiding principles of ethics and ensure human domination of robots, Asimov's stories explore some of the ethical challenges of human/robot interaction.

One of the problems that Asimov explores is the ambiguity of language. In the 1954 story "Conversation with a Commissioner," published in *The Caves of Steel* anthology, a human police officer suggests to a robot justice officer that some laws may be immoral and their enforcement unjust. The robot officer, however, argues that an unjust law is a contradiction. When the human officer suggests the possibility of concepts greater than justice, such as mercy and forgiveness, the robot responds, "I am not acquainted with those words." Asimov thus proposes that robots may not be able to understand the broader cultural, philosophical, and even historical meaning of words such as *justice*.

Unlike science fiction writers before him, Asimov nevertheless saw robotics as promising technology. Indeed, despite the questions Asimov raises in his fiction, according to information technology consultant and cyberlaw and policy professor Roger Clarke, "perhaps ironically, or perhaps because it was artistically appropriate, the sum of Asimov's stories disprove the contention that he began with: It is not possible to reliably constrain the behavior of robots by devising and applying a set of rules."[1] In truth, Clarke argues, Asimov's stories suggest that current managerial, institutional, and legal processes are inadequate for coping with human/robot interaction. Thus, Clarke maintains, robotic engineers and information technology professionals must be sure to address ethical issues. In truth, robotics engineers that explore robot intelligence do in fact debate whether they can develop the software necessary for robots to recognize the nuances of words such as *justice* and, in turn, behave according to human rules of morality or whether human morality will be adequate in a world shared with robots.

One of the great ironies of robotic engineering is that the pursuit of robotic technology, the goal of which is to develop machines that duplicate human skills, behavior, and intelligence so that they might perform in the place of humans, is intimately tied to an understanding of what makes humans human. However, some robotics engineers believe that the distinction between robot and human must remain quite clear. Although the goal for some roboticists is to engineer robots to appear and behave like humans, these robots will not in fact *be* human, and the similarity will create ambiguities that robotics engineers may have to address. Indeed, one of the more controversial theories of robotics is known as the "uncanny valley." This theory, based on a 1970 paper published in the journal *Energy* by Japanese roboticist Masahiro Mori, suggests that while people respond well to human-like robots, there is a tipping point where humans who encounter robots will experience revulsion. Mori provides, as an example, the experience of a human who goes to shake a prosthetic hand, unaware that it is not a human hand. "When we realize the hand, which at first [sight] looked real, is in fact artificial, we experience an eerie sensation. For example, we could be startled during a handshake by its limp boneless grip together with its texture and coldness. When this happens, we lose our sense of affinity, and the hand becomes uncanny." Mori asks that roboticists consider the uncanny valley when developing robots. Instead of creating human-like robots, he recommends that roboticists pursue robots with a moderate degree of human likeness. "We should begin to build an accurate map of the uncanny valley so that through robotics research we can come to understand what makes us human. This map is also necessary to enable us to create—using nonhuman designs—devices to which people can relate comfortably."[2]

Despite Mori's call for research on what makes humans respond with revulsion to some human-like robots, few have studied the phenomena. According to technology journalist and theory critic Erick Sofge, the uncanny valley is more thought experiment and urban legend than true theory. Sofge suggests that "proposing a wide-reaching theory is one thing, but applying any sort of academic rigor to vague notions of familiarity, repulsion and even humanity has shattered the theory into countless smaller ones."[3] Social robotics researcher Kari MacDorman, director of the Android Science Center at Indiana University, suggests a smaller theory, "It's not the overall degree of human likeness that makes [a robot or animated character] uncanny. It's more a matter of mismatch. If you have an extremely realistic skin texture, but at the same time cartoonish eyes, or realistic eyes and an unrealistic skin texture, that's very uncanny."[4] Still other roboticists question the impact of the uncanny valley. Says roboticist David Hanson, "In my experience, people get used to the robots very quickly. . . . As in, within minutes."[5] In the end, reasons Sofge, the uncanny valley is "a largely hypothetical chasm, a term that only partially describes a fleeting, cognitive glitch that has no bearing on the way humans will live with machines."[6]

Both science fiction writers and robotics engineers continue to explore and debate how best to address concerns over increasingly more intimate human/robot interactions. Fictional visions of robot soldiers spur debates over how to create robots that will follow international rules of war. Stories of the challenges of creating robots that make complex judgments and interpret human language inspire discussion over how best to program robot doctors and nurses. Robot narratives also raise questions about what it means to be human and thus *not* a robot. Is it blood and bone, emotion, memory, soul, or even death? The authors of the viewpoints in *Oppos-*

ing Viewpoints: Robotic Technology explore these and other issues in the following chapters: Is Robotic Technology Beneficial?; What Role Should Robotic Technology Play in War?; and What Ethical, Legal, and Moral Issues Relate to Robotic Technology? The controversies surrounding the answers to these questions are part of the study of all new technology and ideas. Indeed, as the late, famed astronomer, exobiologist, and writer Carl Sagan noted, "At the heart of science is an essential balance between two seemingly contradictory attitudes—an openness to new ideas, no matter how bizarre or counterintuitive they may be, and the most ruthless skeptical scrutiny of all ideas, old and new. This is how deep truths are winnowed from deep nonsense."[7] Whether human/robot interactions will have positive outcomes remains to be seen, but many are optimistic. Indeed, most robot engineers have no fear that the artificial intelligence (AI) that will animate the robots of the future will lead to an apocalypse. According to Marvin Minsky, a cognitive scientist, cofounder of Massachusetts Institute of Technology's AI laboratory, and author of several texts on AI and philosophy, "No computer has ever been designed that is ever aware of what it's doing; but most of the time, we aren't either."[8]

Notes

1. Roger Clarke, "Asimov's Laws of Robotics: Implications for Information Technology," *IEEE Computer*, December 1993.

2. Masahiro Mori, "The Uncanny Valley," *IEEE Spectrum*, June 12, 2012. Republished from a 1970 essay in *Energy*. Translated by Karl F. MacDorman and Norri Kageki.

3. Erik Sofge, "The Truth About Robots and the Uncanny Valley," *Popular Mechanics*, June 20, 2010.

4. Quoted in Sofge, "The Truth About Robots and the Uncanny Valley."

5. Quoted in Sofge, "The Truth About Robots and the Uncanny Valley."

6. Sofge, "The Truth About Robots and the Uncanny Valley."

OPPOSING
VIEWPOINTS®
SERIES

CHAPTER 1

Is Robotic
Technology Beneficial?

Chapter Preface

One of several benefits advanced by those who support robotic technology is its potential to respond to both human-made and natural disasters. According to Maryland Robotics Center director Satyandra Gupta, robots are useful when they can perform tasks more consistently and less expensively than humans, when they can perform tasks that humans cannot complete, or when humans can complete the task, but the task is very dangerous. Thus, using robots is appropriate when entering buildings after an earthquake, during a fire, or following a nuclear disaster, as doing so is extremely dangerous for a human being. Robots were in fact used in Japan on March 11, 2011, after a tsunami slammed into the Fukushima No. 1 nuclear power plant, sparking a chain of events that led to a meltdown in reactors 1, 2 and 3. As a result, enormous quantities of exposed radioactive materials prevented workers from going anywhere near the reactors. Two Packbot robots, developed by Massachusetts-based technology firm iRobot Corporation and used primarily by the US military, were first to enter and provide a glimpse inside the buildings. According to advocates, these robots proved invaluable during early efforts to ascertain the full extent of the wreckage inside the units, which suffered huge structural damage as a result of hydrogen explosions. While few doubt the effectiveness of robots in disaster relief, discussion of their use sparks debates over the direction of robotic technology.

Some commentators claim that the focus of robotic technology should be primarily practical. Helen Greiner, one of iRobot Corporation's founders and currently CEO of CyPhy Works, another robotics start-up, asserts, "Merely engineering 'cool' robots does little to advance the field. If robotics is to succeed like computing, what matters is making practical robots that do jobs well and affordably—factors that tend to get lost as people fascinate over the latest autonomous party pieces."

When Japanese policy makers saw how useful the American-made Packbots were in dealing with the nuclear emergency at Fukushima, some began to question the nation's focus on developing humanoid robots that sing, run, and dance. Indeed, Hiroko Nakata reported in the *Japan Times* that many in Japan assumed "that Japan's robotic prowess would play a crucial role in reining in the [nuclear] crisis.", adding, however, that "the nature and focus of Japanese robotic technologies are in sharp contrast to battle-hardened U.S. military robots such as Packbots, which have been deployed countless times on battlefields in Iraq and Afghanistan, and also used to detect radioactive compounds at sites too hazardous for humans to access." Contrary to Greiner's claim, however, Nakata explains that the humanoid robots Japan has developed are designed for more than entertaining. Many Japanese robotic companies are developing robots to help care for the sick. Nevertheless, following the disaster, the Japanese government did in fact budget approximately 1 billion yen to develop robots that can operate in high-radiation surroundings and instructed Tokyo Electric Power (TEPCO), owner of the Fukushima plant, to accelerate work to develop remotely controlled robots.

Other analysts assert that while using robots to help in the event of natural disasters is important, looking at ways to deal with the impact of climate change after the fact is not enough. Some fear that the focus on robotics technology loses sight of the greater problem of climate change, of which the earthquake and subsequent tsunami in Japan is but one example. Those who believe that climate change is due to human impacts such as increased carbon dioxide emissions argue that people must continue to make efforts to reduce greenhouse gases and other human contributions to climate change. According to Tara Holmes of Care2, a social network website that promotes healthy and green living and human rights and environmental activism, "While all of this technology is impressive, we can't lose sight of the bigger picture: these robots aren't designed so we can simply continue business as usual. We instead need to use these new products with the long-term goal of reducing the sources of the problem."

Whether the focus of robotics should be more practical or whether a focus on robotic solutions in the event of natural disaster displaces efforts to address environmental concerns remains controversial. The authors in the following chapter present their views in other debates surrounding the question Is robotic technology beneficial? Despite Holmes's concerns about the human impact on a warming planet and her call to curtail emissions and reduce dependence on fossil fuels, she concedes that robots are "indeed a handy tool until that day comes."

| "If and when (ro)bots develop a high degree of autonomy, simple control systems that restrain inappropriate behavior will not be adequate."

Autonomous Robotic Technology Could Pose a Serious Threat to Humanity

Wendell Wallach and Colin Allen

In the following viewpoint, Wendell Wallach and Colin Allen argue that predicting whether autonomous robots with advanced artificial intelligence will benefit or harm humanity is difficult. However, they reason, assuming that engineers can simply design moral robots is unrealistic. Creating robots in today's moral environment may not prevent unforeseen future consequences, Wallach and Allen assert. Indeed, they maintain, robots with moral restraints might generate robotic offspring that are more likely to survive without these restraints. To gain public support for robotic developments, Wallach and Allen conclude, engineers must ensure that autonomous robots pose no threat to humanity. Wallach is a consultant with Yale University's Interdisciplinary Center for Bioethics. Allen is professor of history and the philosophy of science at Indiana University.

Moral Machines: Teaching Robots Right from Wrong, by Wendell Wallach & Colin Allen (2009), 2714w from Chp. 12 "Dangers, Rights, and Responsibilities," pp.189–190, 191–197. By permission of Oxford University Press, USA. Copyright © 2009 by Wallach & Allen. All rights reserved. Used with permission.

As you read, consider the following questions:

1. According to roboticist Jordan Pollack, as cited by Wallach and Allen, why are self-replicating robots unlikely to post a major threat?

2. What does AI scientist Hugo de Garis think is a potential negative impact of AI research, according to the authors?

3. In the authors' opinion, what might serve as surrogate forms of "punishment" for autonomous robots?

Tomorrow's Headlines:

"Robots March on Washington Demanding Their Civil Rights"

"Terrorist Avatar Bombs Virtual Holiday Destination"

"Nobel Prize in Literature Awarded to IBM's Deep-Bluedora"

"Genocide Charges Leveled at FARL (Fuerzas Armadas Roboticas de Liberacion)"

"Nanobots Repair Perforated Heart"

"VTB (Virtual Transaction Bot) Amasses Personal Fortune in Currency Market"

"UN Debates Prohibition of Self-Replicating AI [artificial intelligence]"

"Serial Stalker Targets Robotic Sex Workers"

Are these headlines that will appear in this century or merely fodder for science fiction writers? In recent years, an array of serious computer scientists, legal theorists, and policy experts have begun addressing the challenges posed by highly intelligent (ro)bots participating with humans in the commerce of daily life. Noted scientists like Ray Kurzweil and Hans Moravec talk enthusiastically about (ro)bots whose intelligence will be superior to that of humans, and how humans will achieve a form of eternal life by uploading their minds into computer systems. Their predictions of the advent of computer systems with intelligence comparable to humans around 2020–50 are based on a computational theory of mind and the projection of Moore's law[1] over the next few decades. Legal scholars debate whether a conscious AI may be designated a "person" for legal purposes, or eventually have rights equal to those of humans. Policy planners reflect on the need to regulate the development of technologies that could potentially threaten human existence as humans have known it. The number of articles on building moral decision-making faculties into (ro)bots is a drop in the proverbial bucket in comparison to the flood of writing addressing speculative future scenarios. . . .

No Robot Rebellion

The futuristic (ro)botic literature spins scenarios of intelligent machines acting as moral or immoral agents, beyond the control of the engineers who built them. (Ro)bots play a pivotal role in both Utopian and dystopian visions.

Speculation that AI systems will soon equal if not surpass humans in their intelligence feed technological fantasies and fears regarding a future robot takeover. Perhaps, as some versions of the future predict, a species of self-replicating (ro)bots will indeed threaten to overwhelm humanity. However, Bill Joy's famous jeremiad in *Wired* (2000) against self-reproducing technology notwithstanding, self-replicating robots are unlikely to be a major threat. The roboticist Jordan Pollack of Brandeis University points out that unlike pathogens or repli-

---

1. Moore's law originally held that the capacity of transistors would double every 18 months. This law was later applied to computational capacity and in the eyes of some can be applied to other technologies.

cating nanotechnology, (ro)bots require significant resources both in the form of raw materials and infrastructure to reproduce themselves. Arresting (ro)bot reproduction is a simple matter of destroying the infrastructure or shutting down the supply chain. Daniel Wilson also captured some of the absurdity in overblown fears of a robot takeover in his dryly humorous yet informative *How to Survive a Robot Uprising: Tips on Defending Yourself Against the Coming Rebellion.*

Nonetheless, tactics for stopping large robots from replicating are not likely to be successful when dealing with tiny nanobots. On the other hand, nanobots, even in this age of miniaturization, are unlikely to be very intelligent. Intelligent or not, the gray goo scenarios beloved by alarmists in which self-replicating nanobots eat all the organic material on earth symbolize the serious ethical challenges posed by nanotechnology. And it is also possible, as Michael Crichton dramatized in his novel *Prey*, that groups of nanobots working together might display threatening swarm behavior.

Confronting the Singularity

Futurists interested in the advent of a Singularity[2] or advanced systems with AGI [artificial general intelligence] commonly refer to the need for friendly AI. The idea of friendly AI is meant to capture the importance of ensuring that such systems will not destroy humanity. However, it is often hard to tell how committed those who speak of this project are to the hard work that would be necessary to make AI friendly, or whether they are giving this project lip service in order to quell the apprehension that advanced AI may not be be-

---

2. The Singularity refers to an event in which an explosive growth in artificial intelligence (AI) exceeds the intelligence of humans. Theorists believe that when AIs come to understand their own construction and see ways to improve themselves, these self-improvements could lead to the singularity. Because humans cannot understand an intelligence beyond their own, predicting the outcome of the singularity is, many reason, impossible.

nign—a fear that might lead to policies that interfere with the headlong charge toward superhuman AI.

The concept of friendly AI was conceived and developed by Eliezer Yudkovsky, a cofounder of the Singularity Institute for AI. The institute assumes that the accelerating development of IT [information technology] will eventually produce smarter-than-human AI and has as its stated goal to confront the opportunities and risks posed by this challenge. Eliezer is a brilliant young man whose ideas sometimes border on genius. He is almost religiously devoted to the belief that a Singularity is inevitable. His thoughts on making AI friendly presume systems will soon have advanced faculties that will facilitate training them to value humans and to be sensitive to human considerations.

Yudkovsky proposes that the value of being "friendly" to humans is *the* top-down principle that must be integrated into AGI systems well before a speculative critical juncture known as the "hard takeoff." As opposed to a "soft takeoff," where the transition to a Singularity takes place over a long period of time, the "hard takeoff" theory predicts that this transition will happen very abruptly, perhaps taking only a few days. The idea is that once a system with near-human faculties turns inward and begins modifying its own code, its development could take off exponentially. The fear is that such a system will soon far exceed humans in its capacities and, if it is not friendly to humans, might treat humans no better than humans treat nonhuman animals or even insects.

Wiring AI with Values

Ben Goertzel does not believe that Yudkovsky's friendly AI strategy is likely to be successful. Goertzel is one of the leading scientists working on building an AGI. His Novamente project is presently directed at building an AGI that functions within the popular online universe Second Life, and he believes that this will be possible within the next decade given adequate funding. Goertzel's concern is that being "friendly" to humans is not likely to be a natural value for an AGI and therefore is less likely to survive successful rounds of self-modification. He proposes that an AGI be designed around a number of basic values. In a working paper on AI morality, Goertzel makes a distinction between those abstract basic values—for example, creating diversity, preserving existing patterns that have proved valuable, and keeping oneself healthy—that might be easy to ground in the system's architecture and hard-to-implement basic values that would need to be learned through experience. Among these "hard basic values" are preserving life and making other intelligent or living systems happy. Without experience, it would be difficult for the system to understand what life or happiness is.

Goertzel suggests that it will be possible to "explicitly wire the AGI with the Easy basic values: ones that are beneficial to humans but also natural in the context of the AGI itself (hence relatively likely to be preserved through the AGI's ongoing self-modification process)," and he advocates the strategy of using "an experiential training approach to give the system the Hard basic values." He properly tempers these suggestions with a dose of humility:

> Finally, at risk of becoming tiresome, I will emphasize one more time that all these remarks are just speculation and intuitions. It is my belief that we will gain a much better practical sense for these issues when we have subhuman but still moderately intelligent AGI's [sic] to experiment with. Until that time, any definitive assertions about the correct route to moral AGI would be badly out of place.

Making Moral Machines

We agree with Goertzel that although it may be important to reflect on serious future possibilities arising from intelligent systems, it will be difficult to make headway on formulating strategies for making those systems moral. First, computer scientists will need to discover which platforms are likely to lead toward a (ro)bot with AGI.

Peter Norvig, director of research at Google and coauthor of the classic modern textbook *Artificial Intelligence: A Modern Approach*, is among those who believe that morality for machines will have to be developed alongside AI and should not be solely dependent on future advances. By now, it should be evident that this is also how we view the challenge of developing moral machines.

Fears that advances in (ro)botic technology might be damaging to humanity underscore the responsibility of scientists to address moral considerations during the development of systems. One AI scientist particularly sensitive to the challenges that advanced AI could pose is Hugo de Garis, who heads the Artificial Intelligence Group at Wuhan University in Wuhan, China. De Garis is working on building brains out of billions of artificial neurons. He has been particularly vocal in pointing out the potential negative impact from AI research, including his own. He foresees a war between those who are supportive of advanced artilects (a term he has derived from "artificial intellects" to refer to ultraintelligent machines) and those who fear artilects.

Nick Bostrom, a philosopher who founded both the World Transhumanist Association and the Future of Humanity Institute at Oxford University, proposes that superintelligent machines will far surpass humans in the quality of their ethical thinking. However, Bostrom cautions that given that such machines would be intellectually superior and unstoppable, it behooves their designers to provide them with human-friendly motivations.

Bostrom, like Josh Storrs Hall, . . . generally holds that superintelligent systems will act in a way that is beneficial to humanity. Michael Ray LaChat of the Methodist Theological School in Ohio goes a step further in predicting the develop-

Avoiding a Robot Apocalypse

[The year 2011 marked] the ninetieth anniversary of the first performance of the play from which we get the term "robot." The Czech playwright Karel Čapek's *R.U.R.* premiered in Prague on January 25, 1921. Physically, Čapek's robots were not the kind of things to which we now apply the term: they were biological rather than mechanical, and humanlike in appearance. But their behavior should be familiar from its echoes in later science fiction—for Čapek's robots ultimately bring about the destruction of the human race....

Some futurists are attempting to take seriously the question of how to *avoid* a robot apocalypse. They believe that artificial intelligence (AI) and autonomous robots will play an ever-increasing role as servants of humanity.... As dependent as we already are on machines, they believe, we should and must expect to be much more dependent on machine intelligence in the future. So we will want to be very sure that the decisions being made ostensibly on our behalf are in fact conducive to our well-being.

Charles T. Rubin,
New Atlantis, *Summer 2011.*

ment of AI into an entity that "will become as morally perfect as human beings can imagine.... The empathetic imagination of this entity will take into account the suffering and pain of all truly sentient beings in the process of decision-making.... Human persons will increasingly come to rely on the moral decisions of this entity." Perhaps, as LaChat's writings suggest, the word "entity" should be replaced with the word "deity."

The Risks of Blind Faith

We do not pretend to be able to predict the future of AI. Nevertheless, the more optimistic scenarios are, to our skeptical minds, based on assumptions that border on blind faith. It is far from clear which platforms will be the most successful for building advanced forms of AI. Different platforms will pose different challenges, and different remedies for those challenges. (Ro)bots with emotions, for example, represent a totally different species from (ro)bots without emotions.

However, we agree that systems with a high degree of autonomy, with or without superintelligence, will need to be provided with something like human-friendly motivations or a virtuous character. Unfortunately, there will always be individuals and corporations who develop systems for their own ends. That is, the goals and values they program into (ro)bots may not serve the good of humanity. Those who formulate public policy will certainly direct attention to this prospect. It would be most helpful if engineers took the potential for misuse into account in designing advanced AI systems.

The development of systems without appropriate ethical restraints or motivations can have far-reaching consequences, even when (ro)bots have been developed for socially beneficial ends. . . . The U.S. Department of Defense is particularly interested in replacing humans in dangerous military enterprises with robots. One stated goal is saving the lives of human soldiers. Presumably, robot soldiers will not be programmed with anything as restrictive as Asimov's First Law.[3] Will, for example, the desirability of saving human lives by building robotic soldiers for combat outweigh the difficulty of guaranteeing that such machines are controllable and can't be misused?

---

3. Science Fiction writer Isaac Asimov posited three laws of robotics: 1) A robot may not harm a human, nor, by inaction allow a human to come to harm. 2) A robot must obey an order from a human, except when that order conflicts with the first law. 3) A robot must protect its own existence, as long as that protection does not conflict with the first or second law.

From the perspective of designing moral machines, the importance of the futuristic scenarios is that they function as cautionary tales, warning engineers to be on guard that solutions to present problems will not hold unintended future consequences. For example, what will happen when military robots come into contact with service robots in a home that have been programmed with Asimov's First Law? Initially, one might assume that very little would change for either the military or the service robot, but eventually, as robots acquired the capacity to reprogram or restructure the way they process information, more serious consequences might result from this meeting, including the prospect that one robot would reprogram the other.

Small, Incremental Changes

In the meantime, the more pressing concern is that very small incremental changes made to structures through which an AMA [artificial moral agent] acquires and processes the information it is assimilating will lead to subtle, disturbing, and potentially destructive behavior. For instance, a robot that is learning about social factors related to trust might overgeneralize irrelevant features, for example eye, hair, or skin color, and develop unwanted prejudices as a result.

Learning systems may well be one of the better options for developing sophisticated AMAs, but the approach holds its own set of unique issues. During adolescence, learning systems will need to be quarantined, sheltering humans from their trials and errors. The better-learning (ro)bots will be open systems—expanding the breadth of information they integrate, learning from their environment, other machines, and humans. There is always the prospect that a learning system will acquire knowledge that conflicts directly with its in-built restraints. Whether an individual (ro)bot will "be conflicted" by such knowledge or use it in a way that circumvents restraints we do not know. Of particular concern is the possibility that a learning system could discover a way to override control mechanisms that function as built-in restraints.

If and when (ro)bots develop a high degree of autonomy, simple control systems that restrain inappropriate behavior will not be adequate. How can engineers build in values and control mechanisms that are difficult, if not impossible, for the system to circumvent? In effect, advanced systems will require values or moral propensities that are integral to the system's overall design and that the system neither can nor would consider dismantling. This was Asimov's vision of a robot's positronic brain being designed around the Three Laws.

The Value of a Bottom-Up Approach

One of the attractions of a bottom-up approach to the design of AMAs is that control mechanisms serving as restraints on the system's behavior might evolve in a manner where they are indeed integrated into the overall design of the system. In effect, integral internal restraints would act like a conscience that could not be circumvented except in pursuit of a goal whose importance to humanity was clear. Storrs Hall and others have stressed this point in favoring the evolutionary approaches for building a conscience for machines. However, bottom-up evolution spawns a host of progeny, and those that adapt and survive will not necessarily be only those whose values are transparently benign from the perspective of humans.

Punishment—from shame to incarceration—or at least fear of punishment plays some role in human development and in restraining inappropriate behavior. Unfortunately, it is doubtful that the notion of being punished would have any lasting effect in the development of (ro)bots. Could a (ro)bot really be designed to *fear* being turned off? Certainly something corresponding to a sense of *failure* or even *shame* might be programmed into a future (ro)botic system to occur if it is unsuccessful at achieving its goals. Furthermore, mechanisms for hampering the system's pursuit of its goals, for example slowing down its information or energy supply if it violates norms, might serve as surrogate forms of "punishment" for simple autonomous (ro)bots. However, more advanced machines will certainly find ways to circumvent these controls to discover their own sources of energy and information.

A Pandora's Box

The restraining influence of authentic feelings of failure or shame suggests the value of a (ro)bot having emotions of its own. Unfortunately, introducing emotions into (ro)bots is a virtual Pandora's box filled with both benefits and ethical challenges. As William Edmonson, a lecturer in the School of Computer Science at the University of Birmingham, writes, "emotionally immature Robots will present humans with strange behaviours and these might raise ethical concerns. Additionally, of course, the Robots themselves may present the ethical challenge—is it unethical to construct Robots with emotions, or unethical to build them without emotions?"

From both a technical and moral perspective, building (ro)bots capable of feeling psychological and physical pain is not a simple matter. . . . While undesirable emotions may play an important role in human moral development, introducing them into (ro)bots for this purpose alone is likely to create many more problems than it solves.

Designing or evolving restraints that are integral to the overall architecture of a (ro)bot is among the more fascinating challenges future roboticists will need to address. Their success in developing adequate control systems may well determine the technological feasibility of designing AMAs, and whether the public will support building systems that display a high degree of autonomy.

"[Machines] can't compose very good songs, write great novels, or generate good ideas for new businesses."

Robots Cannot Duplicate All Human Skills

Erik Brynjolfsson and Andrew McAfee

While digital machines are improving rapidly at advanced pattern recognition and complex human communication, machines cannot duplicate all human skills, particularly those that require creativity and insight, asserts Erik Brynjolfsson and Andrew McAfee in the following viewpoint. Indeed, although computers can conduct legal document reviews more efficiently and even replace some sales personnel, digital machines cannot write good music or come up with original business ventures. Moreover, Brynjolfsson and McAfee reason, digital machines are not yet believably human. Brynjolfsson is director of the Center for Digital Business at the Massachusetts Institute of Technology, and Mc-Afee is a principal research scientist at the center. They also co-authored Race Against the Machine.

As you read, consider the following questions:

1. In a 2011 *New York Times* story by John Markoff, cited by the authors, what was one benefit of moving from human to digital labor during the legal discovery process?

2. According to Brynjolfsson and McAfee, in what way have computers proved to be great pattern recognizers but lousy general problem solvers?

3. In the authors' view, why does the "Turing test" prove that the difference between automatic generation of formulaic prose and genuine insight is still significant?

Although computers are encroaching into territory that used to be occupied by people alone, like advanced pattern recognition and complex communication, for now humans still hold the high ground in each of these areas. Experienced doctors, for example, make diagnoses by comparing the body of medical knowledge they've accumulated against patients' lab results and descriptions of symptoms, and also by employing the advanced subconscious pattern recognition abilities we label "intuition." (*Does this patient seem like they're holding something back? Do they look healthy, or is something off about their skin tone or energy level?*) Similarly, the best therapists, managers, and salespeople excel at interacting and communicating with others, and their strategies for gathering information and influencing behavior can be amazingly complex.

Evidence of Digital Progress

But it's also true that as we move deeper into the second half of the chessboard, computers are rapidly getting better at both of these skills. We're starting to see evidence that this digital progress is affecting the business world. A March 2011 story by John Markoff in the *New York Times* highlighted how heavily computers' pattern recognition abilities are already being exploited by the legal industry where, according to one estimate, moving from human to digital labor during the discovery process could let one lawyer do the work of 500.

In January [2011], for example, Blackstone Discovery of Palo Alto, Calif., helped analyze 1.5 million documents for less than $100,000. . . .

Computers Do Not Get Bored

"From a legal staffing viewpoint, it means that a lot of people who used to be allocated to conduct document review are no longer able to be billed out," said Bill Herr, who as a lawyer at a major chemical company used to muster auditoriums of lawyers to read documents for weeks on end. "People get bored, people get headaches. Computers don't."

The computers seem to be good at their new jobs. . . . Herr . . . used e-discovery software to reanalyze work his company's lawyers did in the 1980s and '90s. His human colleagues had been only 60 percent accurate, he found. "Think about how much money had been spent to be slightly better than a coin toss," he said.

The Retail Industry Is Automating Rapidly

And an article the same month in the *Los Angeles Times* by Alena Semuels highlighted that despite the fact that closing a sale often requires complex communication, the retail industry has been automating rapidly.

In an industry that employs nearly 1 in 10 Americans and has long been a reliable job generator, companies increasingly are looking to peddle more products with fewer employees. . . . Virtual assistants are taking the place of customer service representatives. Kiosks and self-service machines are reducing the need for checkout clerks.

Vending machines now sell iPods, bathing suits, gold coins, sunglasses and razors; some will even dispense prescription drugs and medical marijuana to consumers willing to submit to a fingerprint scan. And shoppers are finding information on touch-screen kiosks, rather than talking to attendants. . . .

The [machines] cost a fraction of brick-and-mortar stores. They also reflect changing consumer buying habits. Online shopping has made Americans comfortable with the idea of buying all manner of products without the help of a salesman or clerk.

Are Any Human Skills Immune?

During the Great Recession, nearly 1 in 12 people working in sales in America lost their job, accelerating a trend that had begun long before. In 1995, for example, 2.08 people were employed in "sales and related" occupations for every $1 million of real GDP [gross domestic product] generated that year. By 2002 (the last year for which consistent data are available), that number had fallen to 1.79, a decline of nearly 14 percent.

If, as these examples indicate, both pattern recognition and complex communication are now so amenable to automation, are any human skills immune? Do people have any sustainable comparative advantage as we head ever deeper into the second half of the chessboard? In the physical domain, it seems that we do for the time being. Humanoid robots are still quite primitive, with poor fine motor skills and a habit of falling down stairs. So it doesn't appear that gardeners and restaurant busboys are in danger of being replaced by machines any time soon.

The Domain of Pure Knowledge

And many physical jobs also require advanced mental abilities; plumbers and nurses engage in a great deal of pattern recognition and problem solving throughout the day, and nurses also do a lot of complex communication with colleagues and patients. The difficulty of automating their work reminds us of a quote attributed to a 1965 NASA report advocating manned space flight: "Man is the lowest-cost, 150-pound, nonlinear, all-purpose computer system which can be mass-produced by unskilled labor."

Even in the domain of pure knowledge work—jobs that don't have a physical component—there's a lot of important territory that computers haven't yet started to cover. In his 2005 book *The Singularity Is Near: When Humans Transcend Biology*, Ray Kurzweil predicts that future computers will "encompass . . . the pattern-recognition powers, problem-solving skills, and emotional and moral intelligence of the human brain itself," but so far only the first of these abilities has been demonstrated. Computers so far have proved to be great pattern recognizers but lousy general problem solvers; IBM's supercomputers, for example, couldn't take what they'd learned about chess and apply it to [the TV game show] *Jeopardy!* or any other challenge until they were redesigned, reprogrammed, and fed different data by their human creators.

Machines Lack Creative Ability

And for all their power and speed, today's digital machines have shown little creative ability. They can't compose very good songs, write great novels, or generate good ideas for new businesses. Apparent exceptions here only prove the rule. A prankster used an online generator of abstracts for computer science papers to create a submission that was accepted for a technical conference (in fact, the organizers invited the "author" to chair a panel), but the abstract was simply a series of somewhat-related technical terms strung together with a few standard verbal connectors.

Similarly, software that automatically generates summaries of baseball games works well, but this is because much sports writing is highly formulaic and thus amenable to pattern matching and simpler communication. Here's a sample from a program called StatsMonkey:

University Park—An outstanding effort by Willie Argo carried the Illini to an 11-5 victory over the Nittany Lions on Saturday at Medlar Field.

Argo blasted two home runs for Illinois. He went 3-4 in the game with five RBIs and two runs scored.

Illini starter Will Strack struggled, allowing five runs in six innings, but the bullpen allowed only no runs and the offense banged out 17 hits to pick up the slack and secure the victory for the Illini.

The difference between the automatic generation of formulaic prose and genuine insight is still significant, as the history of a 60-year-old test makes clear. The mathematician and computer science pioneer Alan Turing considered the question of whether machines could think "too meaningless to deserve discussion," but in 1950 he proposed a test to determine how humanlike a machine could become. The "Turing test" involves a test group of people having online chats with two entities, a human and a computer. If the members of the test group can't in general tell which entity is the machine, then the machine passes the test.

Turing himself predicted that by 2000 computers would be indistinguishable from people 70% of the time in his test. However, at the Loebner Prize, an annual Turing test competition held since 1990, the $25,000 prize for a chat program that can persuade half the judges of its humanity has yet to be awarded. Whatever else computers may be at present, they are not yet convincingly human.

> "Machines are getting so good, so quickly, that they're poised to replace humans across a wide range of industries."

Robotics Increasingly Threatens the Jobs of Human Workers

Farhad Manjoo

Robots work more efficiently, for longer, and are developing their problem-solving skills, claims Farhad Manjoo in the following viewpoint. Thus, he asserts, robots can now perform tasks once performed by highly skilled, well-educated professionals. Although replacing highly skilled labor with machines will reduce costs, Manjoo maintains, it will in turn threaten the livelihoods of those who spent time and money learning these skills. While some believe these workers will find jobs in other industries, others argue that since robotic technology replaces labor, robotic technology will be the exception to this economic principle, he explains. Manjoo, a Wall Street Journal *tech writer, is author of* True Enough: Learning to Live in a Post-Fact Society.

Farhad Manjoo, "Will Robots Steal Your Job? If You're Highly Educated, You Should Still Be Afraid," *Slate*, September 26, 2011. Reproduced by permission.

As you read, consider the following questions:

1. According to Manjoo, what are some of the professions at risk of being replaced by robotic technology?

2. What example does the author provide to show the dark side of the growth of robotic professionals?

3. According to David Autor, as cited by Manjoo, what characteristics do middle-skilled jobs have that make them more likely to be done faster and more cheaply by machines?

If you're taking a break from work to read this article, I've got one question for you: Are you crazy? I know you think no one will notice, and I know that everyone else does it. Perhaps your boss even approves of your Web surfing; maybe she's one of those new-age managers who believes the studies showing that short breaks improve workers' focus. But those studies shouldn't make you feel good about yourself. The fact that you need regular breaks only highlights how flawed you are as a worker. I don't mean to offend. It's just that I've seen your competition. Let me tell you: You are in peril.

A Robot Is Training for Your Job

At this moment, there's someone training for your job. He may not be as smart as you are—in fact, he could be quite stupid—but what he lacks in intelligence he makes up for in drive, reliability, consistency, and price. He's willing to work for longer hours, and he's capable of doing better work, at a much lower wage. He doesn't ask for health or retirement benefits, he doesn't take sick days, and he doesn't goof off when he's on the clock.

What's more, he keeps getting better at his job. Right now, he might only do a fraction of what you can, but he's an indefatigable learner—next year he'll acquire a few more skills, and the year after that he'll pick up even more. Before you know it, he'll be just as good a worker as you are. And soon after that, he'll surpass you.

By now it should be clear that I'm not talking about any ordinary worker. I'm referring to a nonhuman employee—a robot, or some kind of faceless software running on a server. I've spent the last few months investigating the ways in which automation and artificial intelligence are infiltrating a range of high-skilled professions. What I found was unsettling. They might not know it yet, but some of the most educated workers in the nation are engaged in a fierce battle with machines. As computers get better at processing and understanding language and at approximating human problem-solving skills, they're putting a number of professions in peril. Those at risk include doctors, lawyers, pharmacists, scientists, and creative professionals—even writers like myself.

The Rise of the Machines

This is not a new story. People have been fretting about the rise of the machines since Ned Ludd took a hammer to his knitting frames,[1] and probably before. In general, these fears have been unfounded. Yes, better technology sometimes replaces workers in the short run, but over the long march of history, technological improvements have been a key to economic growth, and economic growth improves prospects for workers across a range of industries. Indeed, economists have a name for the popular but misguided notion that technology will displace human workers: They call it the Luddite fallacy, after old Ned himself. To many in the academy, it's an ironclad law of how economies work.

---

1. Ludd was an eighteenth-century Briton who purportedly rebelled against technological progress by attacking the new technology of knitting machines, which had put him out of a job; the term *Luddite* soon came to refer to someone who is antitech or antiprogress.

But this time could be different. Artificial intelligence machines are getting so good, so quickly, that they're poised to replace humans across a wide range of industries. In the next decade, we'll see machines barge into areas of the economy that we'd never suspected possible—they'll be diagnosing your diseases, dispensing your medicine, handling your lawsuits, making fundamental scientific discoveries, and even writing stories just like this one. Economic theory holds that as these industries are revolutionized by technology, prices for their services will decline, and society as a whole will benefit. As I conducted my research, I found this argument convincing—robotic lawyers, for instance, will bring cheap legal services to the masses who can't afford lawyers today. But there's a dark side, too: Imagine you've spent three years in law school, two more years clerking, and the last decade trying to make partner—and now here comes a machine that can do much of your $400-per-hour job faster, and for a fraction of the cost. What do you do now?

The Impact on Middle-Skilled Jobs

There is already some evidence that information technology [IT] has done permanent damage to workers in a large sector of the economy. This specifically applies to workers who are considered "middle skilled," meaning that they need some training, but not much, to do their jobs.

Middle-skilled jobs include many that are generally recognized to be antiquated—secretaries, administrative workers, repairmen, and manufacturing workers, among others. Since the 1980s, across several industrialized nations (including the United States), the number of workers in these job categories has been rapidly declining (the pace of the decline increased greatly during the last recession). Instead, most job growth has been at the poles, in professions that require very high skills and earn high wages, and in the service sector, where most jobs require few skills and pay tiny wages.

Robots in the Workplace

There will be huge job losses by 2040 or 2050 as robots move into the workplace. For example:

- Nearly every construction job will go to a robot. That's about 6 million jobs lost.

- Nearly every manufacturing job will go to a robot. That's 16 million jobs lost.

- Nearly every transportation job will go to a robot. That's 3 million jobs lost.

- Many wholesale and retail jobs will go to robots. That's at least 15 million lost jobs.

- Nearly every hotel and restaurant job will go to a robot. That's 10 million jobs lost.

If you add that all up, it's over 50 million jobs lost to robots. That is a conservative estimate. By 2050 or so, it is very likely that over half the jobs in the United States will be held by robots.

Marshall Brain, Robotic Nation, *2011.*

David Autor, an economist at MIT [the Massachusetts Institute of Technology] who is the leading scholar of this phenomenon, calls it "job polarization." Autor identifies a number of causes for the decline of middle-skilled work, including the decreasing power of unions and the declining federal minimum wage. He puts one factor above the rest, however: The rise of information technology.

Autor argues that middle-skilled jobs tend to have two factors in common—they are composed of lots of tasks that are both routine and geographically portable. What does a secretary do all day? He files, sorts, organizes, watches for calendar conflicts, and in other ways manipulates information. What does a tax preparer do? He asks you a series of questions, and performs some calculations based on your answers. These are all tasks that can be written in software—and, once there, they can be done faster, and more cheaply, by machines. And even when a computer can't completely replace these middle-skilled jobs, it can make them easier to transfer to lower-wage humans—you still need a human being to answer tech support questions, but now you can hire someone in Andra Pradesh [a state in India] rather than Alabama. This decimation of middle-skilled work explains another unsettling trend in American business. New companies today are starting up with far fewer workers than in the past, and they're staying smaller as they grow.

Low- and high-skilled jobs have so far been less vulnerable to automation. The low-skilled jobs categories that are considered to have the best prospects over the next decade—including food service, janitorial work, gardening, home health, childcare, and security—are generally physical jobs, and require face-to-face interaction. At some point robots will be able to fulfill these roles, but there's little incentive to roboticize these tasks at the moment, as there's a large supply of humans who are willing to do them for low wages.

So if computers have already come for middle-skilled workers, and if low-skilled workers aren't an attractive enough target, who's left? That's right: Professionals—people whose jobs required years of schooling, and who, consequently, make a lot of money doing them. As someone who is fascinated with technology, the stuff I found in my investigation of robots and the workforce tickled me. I got to see a room-size pill-dispensing robot, machines that can find cervical cancer on pap-smear slides, and even servers than can write news stories. As someone who likes his job (and his paycheck), what I saw terrified me.

A New Economic Analysis

Most economists aren't taking these worries very seriously. The idea that computers might significantly disrupt human labor markets—and, thus, further weaken the global economy—so far remains on the fringes. The only deep treatment of this story that I've seen has come from a software developer named Martin Ford. In 2009, Ford self-published a small book called *The Lights in the Tunnel: Automation, Accelerating Technology and the Economy of the Future.* In his book, Ford argues persuasively that computers will redefine the very idea of "work" in the modern age.

When I spoke to him recently, I asked Ford about economists' standard rebuttal to fears of automation—the story of the decline of agricultural jobs in the United States. In 1900, 41 percent of the American workforce was employed in agriculture. Over the next 100 years, the technological revolution in farming dramatically increased productivity, enabling fewer and fewer people to produce more and more food. By 2000, just 2 percent of the workforce was employed in agriculture. Yet this shift, which required millions of people to move off farms and acquire new skills, didn't ruin the economy. Instead, by reducing food prices and freeing up people to do more profitable things with their time, it contributed to massive growth. Why won't that happen again with information technology—why won't we all just learn new skills and find other jobs?

"There's no question that there will be new things in the future," Ford says. "But the assumption that economists are making is that those industries are going to be labor-intensive, that there are going to be lots of jobs there. But the fact is we don't see that anymore. Think of all the high-profile companies we've seen over the past 10 years—Google, Facebook, Netflix, Twitter. None of them have very many employees, because technology is ubiquitous—it gets applied everywhere, to new jobs and old jobs. Whatever appears in the future, whatever pops up, we can be certain that IT will get applied right away, and all but the most non-routine-type jobs won't be there anymore."

"Increased levels of automation in front-line medicine are likely to continue . . . [for] there is much that robots and other automated systems have to offer."

Dr. Robot: What Medical Robots Lack in Bedside Manner, They Make Up for in Providing Safer, More Accurate Surgery and Faster Diagnosis of Disease

Ben Hargreaves

In the following viewpoint, Ben Hargreaves asserts that robots can play a valuable role in medicine. For example, remotely operated robots can allow doctors to consult with patients in villages that would otherwise have no doctors, he contends. Originally designed for remote battlefield surgery, remotely operated robots can also perform less-invasive surgical procedures, Hargreaves maintains. In fact, he claims, robot brain surgery allows surgeons to scan the brain while operating. Moreover, he argues,

Ben Hargreaves, "Dr. Robot: What Medical Robots Lack in Bedside Manner, They Make Up for in Providing Safer, More Accurate Surgery and Faster Diagnosis of Disease," *Professional Engineering Magazine*, vol. 24, no. 4, April 2011, pp. 51, 53–54. Reproduced by permission.

robots that operate autonomously reduce costs, allowing patients now on waiting lists to have needed surgery immediately. Hargreaves is deputy editor and blogger at Professional Engineering, *a trade journal.*

As you read, consider the following questions:

1. In Hargreaves's view, why do people in India find robot doctors like the RP-7 appealing?

2. In robotics expert Noel Sharkey's opinion as cited by the author, what type of surgeons might do a better job using robotic assistance?

3. According to Hargreaves, what concerns Sharkey when it comes to robotic surgery?

Medical procedures and interaction with medical professionals are delicate matters. Outstanding healthcare, it could be said, relies as much on the personal touch as on accurate diagnosis and timely treatment. So should we be concerned if robots are now taking over some of the tasks of even high-ranking medical staff such as surgeons?

Increased levels of automation in front-line medicine are likely to continue, the experts say, and while there is a need for stringent checks and balances in the industry, there is much that robots and other automated systems have to offer.

Professor Noel Sharkey, an expert on robotics and the ethics of automated systems at the University of Sheffield, says that criticisms directed at systems such as the RP-7 robot, which can take the place of the doctor at the bedside, are unfounded.

The RP-7, developed by California's InTouch Health, is a mobile robot with a screen through which a doctor at a remote location can converse with a patient. It essentially provides mobile videoconferencing-style services without the need for the patient to be in a room with a laptop, internet connection and webcam, or for the doctor to even be in the same country. Some have criticised the system on the grounds of depersonalization—the bedside manner, or lack of it—but Sharkey believes it has great potential, especially for remote regions in the developing world. He says: "I understand the concern that it is very important not to deprive people of contact with their surgeon or doctor. By contact, we mean personal visual contact to relieve anxiety—that's a big thing.

"But in the case of the RP-7, which comes and talks to you, that's a little bit short-sighted. If you look a little bit into the future of these systems, what they mean is you can talk to several doctors through it." Remote areas in emerging economies that have little or no access to doctors could benefit from similar technology. Sharkey says: "I have given talks in India where I talk about service robots in general, and they laugh at the idea of cleaning robots and that sort of thing because there's so much manpower.

"But what they don't laugh at is the idea of travelling robot doctors like the RP-7. It's not really a doctor, it's just a device that lets the doctor speak, and there is such a shortage of doctors in India: there are many, many villages that have no doctors at all."

Surgery is also an area where automation has made significant inroads over the past decade. Prime among these systems is the da Vinci surgical system, developed by US firm Intuitive Surgical, which is currently being used at 22 hospitals in Britain. The da Vinci system was originally developed with military needs in mind and designed to assist surgeons carrying out laparoscopic, or minimally invasive, "keyhole" surgery. Chris Simmonds, senior director of marketing services at Intuitive Surgical, says: "The original prototype for Intuitive Surgical's da Vinci system was developed in the late 1980s at the former Stanford Research Institute under contract to the US Army.

"While initial work was funded in the interest of developing a system for performing battlefield surgery remotely, possible commercial applications were even more compelling: it was clear to those involved that this technology could accelerate the application of a minimally invasive surgical approach to a broader range of procedures."

The US Food and Drug Administration approved the da Vinci for general laparoscopic surgery in 2000. In subsequent years it has been approved for thoracoscopic (chest) surgery, cardiac procedures with adjunctive incisions, urologic, gynaecologic, paediatric, and trans-oral otolaryngology (ear, nose and throat) procedures. It was first used in Britain at St Mary's Hospital, Paddington, London, for cardiovascular treatments, and is still in use there today.

The da Vinci system has opened up some operations such as the removal of the prostate to minimally invasive surgery, with an increase in the number of these operations in the US being performed using laparoscopic techniques by surgeons employing it. Benefits of minimally invasive surgery include less pain, fewer complications and quicker recovery times for patients.

Sharkey is clear that automation can pay dividends in the complex arena of surgery. He says: "I've heard it said that surgeons should be able to do these jobs just as well as robots. But those I've talked to say that, while that might be the case with the top surgeons, it's not always that way.

"The top surgeons can do as well as a robot—maybe even better. But there are more junior surgeons where, potentially, they would do a better job using robotic assistance."

Systems like the da Vinci, he says, "allow the surgeon to delineate the area inside where he or she goes". He adds: "It stops them making big sweeps and sets a boundary. But also you can make big hand movements outside the body, and the system makes tiny little hand movements inside—so if you

A Neurally Controlled Robotic Arm

It's October [2008] at Duke University, in Durham, N.C., and Jonathan Kuniholm is playing "air guitar hero," a variation on *Guitar Hero*, the Nintendo Wii game that lets you try to keep up with real musicians using a vaguely guitarlike controller. But the engineer is playing without a guitar. More to the point, he's playing without his right hand, having lost it in Iraq in 2005. Instead he works the controller by contracting the muscles in his forearm, creating electrical impulses that electrodes then feed into the game. After about an hour he beats the high score set by Robert Armiger, a two armed Johns Hopkins University engineer who modified *Guitar Hero* to train amputees to use their new prostheses.

Armiger's research is part of a nationwide effort to create a neurally controlled prosthetic arm.

Sally Adee,
Spectrum, *January 2009.*

jerk your hand suddenly it's not going to jerk with you. It really is very useful for a lower skill level, extremely useful.

I suppose therefore that, speaking ethically, it should be used. Anything that's going to make the patient's life easier should be used. But on the proviso that the doctor's always there: that they can meet the doctor.

Other robotic innovations are taking place in brain surgery. One such is Canada's Neuro Arm, which is a robot specifically designed for neurosurgery that was launched. It allows the surgeon to operate remotely on the patient's brain while accessing a near-realtime magnetic resonance imaging (MRI) feed—as the system can fit inside a scanner.

The surgeon seated at the workstation controls the robot using force feedback hand controllers to provide a sense of touch and the robot's "end effectors" interface with standard surgical instruments. Because of the ability to scan the brain while operating, surgeons can perform common neurological procedures such as biopsy and the manipulation of soft tissue. Outside of the MRI, the system is dexterous enough to perform microsurgery.

British machine tool firm Renishaw has also been looking at the potential of robotic systems for surgery, as well as automated systems for the diagnosis of illness [see box (not shown)], as it expands into medical markets. Dr George Boukouris, of the company's Neurological Products Division, says its key product, a robot called the Neuromate, builds upon Renishaw's expertise in measurement technologies. It can, he says, improve the accuracy of brain surgery by about 0.3mm, replacing the need for traditional stereotactic frames—a technology that is some 60 years old.

"To give you an idea of the level of accuracy using stereotactic frames," Boukouris says, "a surgeon would typically be looking at an accuracy of 0.8mm to the target. He could expect through the robot to get to 0.5mm. Sometimes he'll be able to get to 0.5 manually—but the surgeon wants to be able to do that every time. So what the robot brings to the situation is repeatability, stability and accuracy, which should make surgery safer. In effect we're automating an element of the process."

In general, Sharkey believes these trends in automation are welcome and are predicated on what they should be: the welfare of the patient. He says: "The Neuro Arm I would describe as a major breakthrough for surgeons because of what it allows you to do in terms of scanning and surgery simultaneously. It really is remarkable."

He believes a future in which semi-autonomous or even completely autonomous robots carry out routine surgical procedures is possible. It might even be the case that, one day, lower-ranking medical staff than surgeons are left to supervise them. "Ethically, it could be a good thing. We have long waiting lists for operations, and by using machines we could do more of them, and with a faster turnover."

But he cautions: "There would be some concerns of 'conveyor belt' surgery developing, without the personal interaction that we like with our doctors and surgeons."

More ominously, he warns: "Lower level people than surgeons being able to supervise operations should be a good thing but, on the bad side, you need to make sure that whoever's there can cope when something goes wrong.

"Quite often, a medical emergency, a surgical emergency, needs to be dealt with within seconds."

> *"Robots cannot advocate for patients and correct the surgeon who is removing a gallbladder instead of removing a pancreatic tumor."*

Robot Nurses Cannot Replace Human Nurses

Rebecca Hendren

Although robots may be able to perform some tasks performed by surgical nurses, they cannot replace them, argues Rebecca Hendren in the following viewpoint. Surgical nurses, also known as scrub nurses, do much more than hand instruments to surgeons during surgery, she asserts. In fact, Hendren reports, unlike robots, human nurses can note changes in patients that indicate they might be in trouble during surgery. Human nurses can also recognize and correct physician errors or prevent intoxicated surgeons from operating, she explains. Hendren, managing editor for HCPro, Inc., a multimedia health care education and training provider, manages HCPro's Leaders' Lounge blog.

As you read, consider the following questions:

1. According to Hendren, what did the response to the implication that "nurse" robots could replace scrub nurses illustrate about the nursing profession?

2. How do TV programs such as *ER* and *Grey's Anatomy* portray the role of nurses, in the author's view?

3. In Hendren's opinion, what results when the public does not understand what nurses do?

An article about robotic technology caused a minor controversy last week [in February 2011] when it appeared to imply that "nurse" robots could replace scrub nurses. The flurry of emails and discussion it generated illustrates the nursing profession's perception problems.

The seemingly innocuous piece discussed fascinating hand gesture recognition technology developed by Juan Pablo Wachs, assistant professor of industrial engineering, and others at Purdue University.

Visual recognition technology has previously been the purview of science fiction. With Wachs' prototype, it's potentially a few short years away from implementation in operating rooms around the country.

The creators say the robot can recognize surgeons' visual cues to pass instruments or recognize commands to display data during surgeries. The hope is that robots may reduce length of surgeries and potential for infection.

Robots may eventually perform some tasks now performed by scrub nurses, such as handing surgeons instruments. That's where the debate begins. The article describes the high-tech machines as "robotic scrub nurses" and Wachs discusses the advantages the machines have over human scrub nurses when working with unfamiliar surgeons, for example.

It didn't take long for nurses to complain to me about the use of the term "nurse" and the implications that robots could replace humans.

Misperceptions About Nursing

First, let's look at the use of the term.

"There's a lot of power in a name," says Kathleen Bartholomew, speaker, author, consultant, and nurse. "The real problem is that the casual use of the word in this way validates what we already know—which is that the general public doesn't know what we do."

Bartholomew believes misrepresentation undervalues and damages the profession. That leads to the second point that nurses may be replaced by a machine. At first glance, this is laughable. Outside of science fiction, no one believes machines can replace humans.

"Robots cannot detect subtle changes in patients before they crash and intervene to save their lives," says Sandy Summers, RN, MSN, MPH, founder and executive director of The Truth About Nursing, an advocacy group that works to counter misrepresentations of nursing in the media. "Robots cannot advocate for patients and correct the surgeon who is removing a gallbladder instead of removing a pancreatic tumor, because he forgot which patient this was. Robots cannot eject drunk surgeons from the operating room."

The nurses I spoke with cite the discussion of the robot scrub "nurse" as evidence of the commonly-held belief that nursing is merely a collection of tasks that can be completed by anybody. According to TV programs like *ER* and *Grey's Anatomy*, nurses are invisible minions who carry out low-skilled tasks such as emptying bed pans and bringing food trays. While everyone who works in healthcare knows these portrayals are inaccurate, even within healthcare the role of nursing is frequently misunderstood and undervalued.

Furthermore, the public doesn't understand the value that nurses provide to patients and healthcare teams. They do not see the role of nurses as critical to safety because there are no true-to-life examples in the media.

A Need for Public Education

If the public doesn't understand what nurses do, then nursing priorities do not get resources allocated. Bartholomew cited the proposed reductions of the nursing workforce development programs and health professions funding by 29% over fiscal year 2010, which are before Congress. These resources are desperately needed to ease the chronic faculty shortage in nursing schools and to open more spaces to educate students so that we have enough nurses to meet the looming nurse shortfall created by the inevitable aging baby boomers.

"Clearly the general public doesn't know what nurses do," says Bartholomew. "It's easy to understand why for two reasons. One, we don't tell them. Nurses don't sit around bragging about how they saved someone's life or intercepted a potential physician error or broke the news to a mother that her baby was not going to live. We don't talk about these things amongst ourselves, let alone the general public. And the second reason is because of the obvious mis-portrayal of nurses in the media."

When a profession is misunderstood and undervalued, it does not reach its potential. In the era of healthcare reform, we need nurses—fully-engaged, well-educated, skilled professionals with vigilant observational and critical thinking skills—to meet the needs of our patients.

| "Human space exploration has a number of advantages over robotic operations."

Humans Are More Productive than Robots for Space Exploration

Ian A. Crawford

In the following viewpoint, Ian A. Crawford asserts that humans provide several benefits over robot space explorers; for example, he maintains, humans have greater mobility and therefore more opportunities to explore. Moreover, Crawford claims, humans perform tasks more quickly than robots. The greatest advantage is that human space missions are designed to bring the explorers and their samples back to Earth, he argues. In truth, Crawford reasons, when considering the savings in mobility and efficiency, the cost of human space exploration is not as significant as some claim. Crawford is in the Department of Earth and Planetary Science at Birkbeck College in London.

As you read, consider the following questions:

1. What data does Crawford provide to support his claim that the enhanced mobility of humans makes humans better explorers?

Ian A. Crawford, "Dispelling the Myth of Robotic Efficiency," *Astronomy and Geophysics*, vol. 53, no. 2, April 2012, pp. 2.22–2.26. Reproduced by permission of Oxford University Press.

2. According to the author, why is tele-robotic exploration more efficient than autonomous robotic operation?

3. What evidence does the author provide regarding the reduction of the cost ratio of the Apollo and Mars Science Laboratory missions?

There is a widely held view in the astronomical community that unmanned robotic space vehicles are, and always will be, more efficient explorers of planetary surfaces than astronauts. Partly this comes from a common assumption that robotic exploration is *cheaper* than human exploration (although this isn't necessarily true if like is compared with like) and partly from the expectation that developments in technology will relentlessly increase the capability and reduce the size and cost of robotic missions to the point that human exploration will not be able to compete. I argue below that the experience of human exploration during the Apollo missions, more recent field analogue studies and trends in robotic space exploration all point to exactly the opposite conclusion.

The Benefits of Human Space Exploration

As demonstrated by the Apollo missions 40 years ago—and leaving the question of cost to a separate examination below—human space exploration has a number of advantages over robotic operations on planetary surfaces. These ... were endorsed by the independent Commission on the Scientific Case for Human Space Exploration commissioned by the RAS [Royal Astronomical Society] in 2005. These advantages can be summarized as follows:

- On-the-spot decision making and flexibility, with increased opportunities for serendipitous discoveries.

- Greatly enhanced mobility and attendant opportunities for geological exploration and instrument deployment. Compare the 35.7 km traversed in three days by the

Apollo 17 astronauts in December 1972 with the almost identical distance (34.4 km) traversed by the Mars Exploration Rover *Opportunity* in eight years.

- Greatly increased efficiency in sample collection and sample return capacity. Compare the 382 kg of samples returned by Apollo with the 0.32 kg from the Russian robotic sample return missions Lunas 16, 20 and 24, and the zero kg returned so far by any robotic mission to Mars.

- Increased potential for large-scale exploratory activities (e.g. drilling) and the deployment and maintenance of complex equipment.

- The development of a space-based infrastructure to support space-based astronomy and other scientific applications (e.g. the construction and maintenance of large space telescopes).

Comparing Efficiency

With the exception of the final point, for which the best demonstration is provided by the five successful space shuttle servicing missions to the Hubble Space Telescope, demonstration of the benefits of human space-flight for planetary exploration must be sought in a comparison of the relative efficiencies of the Apollo missions and robotic missions to the Moon and Mars, supported where appropriate with terrestrial analogue studies.

The relative efficiency of human over robotic exploration of planetary surfaces is well recognized by scientists directly involved with the latter. For example, regarding the exploration of Mars, the RAS Report (paragraph 70) noted:

The expert evidence we have heard strongly suggests that the use of autonomous robots alone will very significantly limit what can he learned about our nearest potentially habitable planet.

63

Putting it more bluntly, Steve Squyres, the PI [principal investigator] for the Mars Exploration Rovers (MERs) *Spirit* and *Opportunity*, has written:

> "[t]he unfortunate truth is that most things our rovers can do in a perfect sol [i.e., a Martian day] a human explorer could do in less than a minute."

This is of course only a qualitative assessment, albeit by someone well-placed to make an informed judgement. Nevertheless, at face value it implies a human/robot efficiency ratio of about 1,500, which is far larger than the likely ratio of cost between a human mission to Mars and the cost of the MERs (see below). Even this, however, does not fairly compare human exploration efficiency with robotic exploration. This is because much of the scientific benefit of human missions will consist of samples returned, drill cores drilled and geophysical instruments deployed, all of which were demonstrated by Apollo on the Moon, but none of which have been achieved by the MERs nor will be achieved by the more capable (and vastly more expensive) Mars Science Laboratory (MSL) that is due to land on Mars in 2012.[1]

Objective Estimates

More objective estimates of the relative efficiency of robots and humans as field geologists have been given by [J.] Garvin [in the journal *Earth Moon Planets* in 2004] and [K.] Snook *et al.* [in the 2007 book *The Geology of Mars*]. Garvin summarized the results of a NASA [National Aeronautics and Space Administration] survey of several dozen planetary scientists and engineers on the relative efficiency of human and robotic capabilities in 18 different skill sets relevant to planetary exploration. The results . . . show a clear balance in favour of human capabilities (with the implicit recognition that the

1. The mission successfully landed the rover *Curiosity* on Mars on August 5, 2012.

most efficient exploration strategies of all will be those consisting of human-robotic partnerships where each complements the other).

This conclusion is corroborated by direct field comparisons of human and robotic exploration at planetary analogue sites on Earth. Snook *et al.* reported the results of one such study, conducted at the Haughton impact crater in the Canadian Arctic, where the efficiency of a human explorer (suitably encumbered in a spacesuit) was compared with that of a tele-operated rover (controlled from NASA Ames Research Centre in California) in the performance of a range of exploration tasks. The rover was more sophisticated than those employed in present-day space missions, and included simulation of artificial intelligence capabilities that are only likely to be incorporated in actual space missions from 2015 at the earliest. Nevertheless, the space-suited "astronaut" was found to be much more efficient in performing exploration tasks than the rover, and Snook *et al.* concluded that "humans could be one to two orders of magnitude [an order of magnitude equals ten times more] more productive per unit of time in exploration than future terrestrially controlled robots".

Although this estimate is an order of magnitude lower than Squyres' off-the-cuff estimate of 1,500 given above, this is mainly because the comparison was conducted between human and *tele-robotic* exploration, rather than between humans and supervised quasi-autonomous robotic exploration such as carried out by the MERs and MSL. Tele-robotic exploration is known to be more efficient than autonomous robotic operation, precisely because real-time human interaction is involved, but it cannot be employed effectively on planetary surfaces more distant than the Moon because of the inevitable communications delay. Garvin has compared the efficiencies of robotic, tele-robotic, and human exploration, from which it is clear that if humans are "one to two orders of magnitude more efficient" than tele-robots then they will be even *more*

Space for Both Humans and Robots

The common assumption is that ... if you support ro-bots, you are against human exploration and vice versa. ... That just isn't so. There are plenty of people who do robotic exploration work like myself, who are very strong supporters of human exploration. I mean that's what got me and many of my colleagues into the business in the first place. You know, watching guys bounce around on the moon, watching people in Skylab and in space shuttle. And you know those are the adventures, those are the human interest stories, those are the dramas that capture the attention of the public and the kids who eventually are going to go on to get into these kinds of science and engineering fields. And so ... just because you are for robotic exploration, doesn't mean you are against human exploration.

Jim Bell, Scientific American, *July 18, 2007.*

efficient when compared with robotic vehicles such as the MERs or MSL, bringing the two estimates into better agreement.

Returning to Earth

Moreover, while comparisons based on the relative time taken to perform certain tasks do indeed show humans to be more efficient than robots, they nevertheless grossly underestimate the added scientific value of having humans on planetary surfaces. This is because astronauts have to come back to Earth, and can therefore bring large quantities of intelligently collected samples back with them. Robotic explorers, on the other hand, generally do not return—one reason why they are cheaper—so nothing can come back with them. Even if robotic sample return missions are implemented, neither the quantity nor the diversity of these samples will be as high as would be achievable in the context of a human mission— again compare the 382 kg of samples (collected from more than 2,000 discrete locations) returned by Apollo, with the 0.32 kg (collected from three locations) brought back by the Luna sample return missions. The Apollo sample haul might also be compared with the ≤0.5 kg generally considered in the context of future robotic Mars sample return missions. Note that this comparison is not intended in any way to down-play the scientific importance of robotic Mars sample return, which will in any case be essential before human missions can responsibly be sent to Mars, but merely to point out the step change in sample availability (both in quantity and diversity) that may be expected when and if human missions *are* sent to the planet. . . .

Human Exploration Costs

Although it is generally taken for granted that human explo-ration is more expensive than robotic exploration, and this is certainly true if the aggregate costs are the only ones consid-ered, the situation is not as clear cut as it is sometimes made out to be. For one thing, the ratio of costs between human and robotic missions, while large, may nevertheless be smaller than the corresponding ratio in scientific productivity. The Apollo missions are instructive in this respect. [D.E.] Wil-helms [in the 1993 book *To the Rocky Moon*] and [D.A.] Beat-tie [in the 2001 book *Taking Science to the Moon*] estimated a total cost of Apollo as $25bn "in 1960s money". This is rather more than the Congressional appropriations for Apollo ($19.4bn from 1961 to 1973). Taking the higher estimate (to be conservative) and taking "1960s" to be 1966 when Apollo expenditure peaked, this corresponds to about $175bn today.

It is interesting to compare this with the cost of a modern state-of-the-art robotic mission such as the Mars Science Laboratory. MSL . . . has cost an estimated $2.5bn. Thus, in real terms, Apollo cost 70 times as much as MSL. However, Apollo visited six sites, whereas MSL will visit one. In terms of cost-per-site Apollo was only 12 times dearer than MSL, yet each Apollo mission was vastly more capable. It is true that this comparison only strictly holds in the context of lunar exploration, where we can compare Apollo with a hypothetical future MSL-like lunar rover. In the context of Mars exploration, human missions seem likely to be more expensive than Apollo in real terms, although not necessarily by a large factor. The estimated total costs of some human Mars mission architectures are comparable to that of Apollo, or even lower. The main point is that human missions like Apollo are between two and three orders of magnitude more efficient in performing exploration tasks than robotic missions, while being only one to two orders of magnitude more expensive. In addition, human missions can accomplish scientific objectives that are unlikely to be achieved robotically at all (deep drilling and properly representative sample collection and return are obvious examples, as well as the increased opportunities for serendipitous discoveries). Looked at this way, human space exploration doesn't seem so expensive after all!

That said, there is a more sophisticated and productive way to view the relative costs of human and robotic spaceflight. The fact is that while robotic planetary missions are science-focused, and essentially their whole costs are therefore borne by scientific budgets, human spaceflight is not wholly, or even mainly, science-driven. Rather, the ultimate drivers of human spaceflight tend to be geopolitical concerns, industrial development and innovation, and employment in key industries. Thus, science can be a beneficiary of human missions instituted and (largely) paid for by other constituencies. Apollo again provides an excellent example: it was instituted for geopolitical rather than scientific reasons, and to first order the US government's expenditure of $25bn ($175bn today) would have occurred anyway, whether any science was performed or not. Fortunately, owing largely to the efforts of a relatively small number of senior scientists scientific objectives and capabilities were incorporated into Apollo and resulted in the rich scientific legacy that is still being exploited today. . . .

A Way Forward

The lesson seems clear: if at some future date a series of Apollo-like human missions return to the Moon and/or are sent on to Mars, and if these are funded (as they will be) for a complex range of socio-political reasons, scientists will get more for our money piggy-backing science on them than we will get by relying on dedicated autonomous robotic vehicles which will, in any case, become increasingly unaffordable.

Fortunately, there is a way forward. In 2007 the world's space agencies came together to develop the Global Exploration Strategy (GES), which lays the foundations for a global human exploration programme that could provide us with just such an opportunity. One of the first fruits of the GES has been the development of a Global Exploration Roadmap (GER 2011), which outlines possible international contributions to human missions to the Moon, near-Earth asteroids and, eventually, Mars. The motivations for the GES are, needless-to-say, multifaceted, and include a range of geopolitical and societal motivations (many of them highly desirable in themselves) in addition to science.

Science would be a major beneficiary of participating in a human exploration programme such as envisaged by the Global Exploration Strategy. Quite simply, this will result in new knowledge, including answers to fundamental questions regarding the origin and evolution of planets, and the distribution and history of life in the solar system, that will not be obtained as efficiently, and in many cases probably not obtained at all, by reliance on robotic exploration alone.

"A [space exploration] mission including humans would be vastly more complicated than a robot mission, and a
more complicated mission has many
more possible failure points."

Robots Are as Effective as Humans for Space Exploration

Chad Orzel

Claims that humans are better space explorers than robots give too much credit to humans and too little to robots, argues Chad Orzel in the following viewpoint. Robots are just as capable of making unexpected discoveries as humans are, he maintains. Moreover, Orzel asserts, psychology shows that humans often miss important details. Robots may encounter problems that a human might easily fix, he concedes, but complex problems challenge even humans. In the end, Orzel reasons, robot space exploration is less costly. Orzel, professor of physics at Union College in Schenectady, New York, blogs about physics and is author of How to Teach Physics to Your Dog.

As you read, consider the following questions:

1. What example does Orzel give to prove his claim that Mars rovers are capable of serendipitous discoveries?

Chad Orzel, "Exploring Space: Don't Sell Robots Short," ScienceBlogs.com, May 9, 2012. Reproduced by permission.

2. What does the author claim is true of more complicated human space missions?

3. What does the author claim is the one unquestionable advantage of a human Mars mission?

One of the things I found really frustrating about the book [*Space Chronicles: Facing the Ultimate Frontier*], and the whole argument that we ought to be sinking lots of money into manned space missions is that the terms of the argument are so nebulous. This is most obvious when [author Neil de-Grasse] Tyson or other space advocates talk about the need for "inspiring" people, but it shows up even in what ought to be relatively concrete discussions of actual science.

Selling Robots Short

Take, for example, the argument over humans vs. robots. Given the success of the robotic missions to Mars and other bodies, many people ask why we should bother to send people to any of those places. Tyson himself estimates the cost of sending a human to be around fifty times the cost of sending a robot, and says that "if my only goal in space is to do science, and I'm thinking strictly in terms of the scientific return on my dollar, I can think of no justification for sending a person into space." But then, he turns around and tries to justify it on fairly standard grounds: that humans are more flexible, while a robot can only "look for what it has already been programmed to find." Having humans on the scene would enable faster and more "revolutionary" discoveries.

This is an argument that sounds fairly convincing on a surface level, but on closer inspection it breaks down in two ways: it's too generous to humans, and too hard on the robots.

One line of argument in favor of sending humans is that, being autonomous multi-function life forms, humans can notice things that robots wouldn't, and adjust accordingly—

Tyson cites the example of Apollo 17 astronaut Harrison Schmitt, a geologist by training, noticing some oddly colored soil that turned out to be interesting after he sampled it. The claim being that a robot, following a strict program, would not be able to adjust on the fly and sample that soil rather than some other soil.

Which would be true, if we were dealing with Apollo-era robot technology. But we're not. In fact, the actual existing robot rovers on Mars have the capability to do exactly what he wants: they send back pictures of the surface of Mars to Earth, where human geologists study them. Based on the pictures, they select what targets to investigate on more or less the same criteria Schmitt used: that rock is an interesting-looking shape, or this spot is a different color than that other spot. That's been the beauty of the robot rover program from the beginning.

And, in fact, if you go down the list of discoveries made by the Mars rovers, a large number of them have been serendipitous in exactly the manner that you're supposed to be able to get from a human. The hematite "blueberries," for example: scientists on Earth looking at the pictures sent back by *Opportunity* saw some odd little spherules on the ground, and directed the robot to investigate.

Overselling Human Exploration

This also oversells human ability a bit—by definition, serendipitous discoveries have an element of chance. There's no guarantee that even a human geologist would happen to notice everything interesting. In fact, tons of psychology research has shown that humans are just as susceptible to not noticing things as robots are supposed to be—people miss gorillas right in front of them, after all. A human geologist on Mars with limited time to work might well miss some things that would turn out to be interesting.

"Surf's Up," cartoon by Bob Englehart, *Hartford Courant*, December 8, 2006. Copyright © 2006 by Bob Englehart and Cagle Cartoons.

Another branch of the flexibility argument holds that humans could move more quickly past problems—Tyson cites the 12 hours that it took to navigate [the rover] *Spirit* past the airbag from its lander, and says that a human could've cleared it in seconds—and make on-the fly repairs—"Give a person a wrench, a hammer, and some duct tape, and you'd be surprised what can get fixed," he says. This again, is true to a point, but also elides a lot. For one thing, a mission including humans would be vastly more complicated than a robot mission, and a more complicated mission has many more possible failure points. So, yes, a human is less likely to be thwarted by an airbag on a ramp, but then a robot doesn't have to worry about maintaining a pressurized breathable atmosphere, or securing supplies of food and water, or a comfortable temperature, or adequate radiation shielding, or waste disposal, or any of a host of other problems that preserving human scientists on Mars and returning them to Earth would entail. There are lots of possible failures that are just as stupid as an airbag on a ramp that could easily trap a human inside for as long as *Spirit* was stuck.

The repair argument also has its flaws, the most obvious being that any repairs would be limited by the available materials. Glib's comments about duct tape are great if the only failures you worry about are gross mechanical ones, but nobody's going to make a new Mössbauer spectrometer out of duct tape. Any Mars mission worth doing will include a lot of highly specialized components, and you can't send spares of everything.

It also slights the ingenuity of the humans controlling the robots. *Spirit* famously had one of its wheels lock up in 2006, but the scientists "driving" it not only worked out a way to get around the stuck wheel (by driving the rover "backwards," basically), but it turned out to be the vehicle for another of those serendipitous discoveries: the dragging wheel scraped away dust, revealing a silica layer underneath.

Small Advantages, High Price

So, again, a lot of what appear to be more concrete arguments in favor of human space missions don't seem to hold up very well, and end up turning on things that are as vague and unquantifiable as "inspiration." There's no question that certain things would go faster for humans than they do for robots, but then, they would *need* to go faster, because there's no way we'd be able to leave a human on Mars for the nearly 3,000 "sols" [Martian days] that the current robot rovers have been operating there. And it's not at all clear that the small advantage in flexibility from having a human there rather than at the other end of a radio link would make a positive difference.

The one unquestionable advantage would be that a mission putting humans on Mars would eventually return to Earth, and could bring samples back that could then be subjected to a vast range of tests that can't be done by a robot rover with a limited instrument set. Which is true, but then, you could get the same thing from a robotic sample return mission, at one-fiftieth the price.

So, while the pro-human arguments based on science sound convincing at first, they're ultimately not that great, and fall back on the same sort of vague and airy platitudes as the general "inspiration" argument. And given the gigantic cost multiplier involved in sending humans rather than robots (or in addition to robots), I'd really like to see more than that.

Periodical and Internet Sources Bibliography

The following articles have been selected to supplement the diverse views presented in this chapter.

Marshal Brain	"Robotic Nation," 2011. www.marshallbrain.com.
Sal Gentile	"From Watson to Siri: As Machines Replace Humans Are They Creating Inequality Too?," Public Broadcasting Service, October 25, 2011. www.pbs.org.
Alexandra Godfrey	"What's New in Minimally Invasive Surgery: Robotic Technology Speeds Recovery and Improves Outcomes," *Journal of the American Academy of Physician Assistants*, October 21, 2010.
C. Gopinath	"When Robots Replace People at the Workplace," *Hindu Business Line*, February 26, 2012. www.thehindubusinessline.com.
Helen Greiner	"Time for Robots to Get Real," *New Scientist*, January 21, 2012.
Satyandra Gupta, as told to Rachel Ehrenberg	"We, Robot: What Real-life Machines Can and Can't Do," *Science News*, October 9, 2010. www.sciencenews.org.
William Lazonick	"Robots Don't Destroy Jobs; Rapacious Corporate Executives Do," AlterNet, December 31, 2012. www.alternet.org.
Space Daily	"Finding ET May Require Giant Robot Leap," May 2, 2012. www.spacedaily.com.
Alice G. Walton	"The Robots of Medicine: Do the Benefits Outweigh the Costs?," *Atlantic Monthly*, March 2012.

OPPOSING
VIEWPOINTS®
SERIES

CHAPTER 2

What Role Should Robotic Technology Play in War?

Chapter Preface

While walking the perimeter of a Marine camp in Iraq, Marine Corps General James Mattis, at the time head of US Joint Forces Command and NATO Transformation, came upon six Marines in formation with a small American flag. These Marines were part of an explosive ordnance disposal (EOD) team, and they were burying the remains of a robot that disarmed bombs—giving the robot a full military honors funeral. "They said it took six wounds. 'We were able to put it back together six times, but it was blown up, and this time, as you can see, there's nothing left,'" Mattis recounts. Although the incident might sound like a practical joke, "that robot had saved their lives," Mattis asserts. "It had crawled up next to bombs how many times and they had actually developed a fondness that oftentimes you develop for your shipmates when you're in tough times," he explains. In the case of bomb disposal robots, the life-saving function is clear. Few question the ethics of their use. Less clear, however, are the ethical considerations surrounding unmanned aerial vehicles, also known as drones, which are operated by a pilot some seventy-five hundred miles away and that kill combatants and noncombatants alike. Indeed, as robots play an ever-increasing role in US military operations, one of several controversies that have arisen is whether soldiers operating these robots will become too disconnected from the battlefield.

The US military has clearly embraced robots, although many were skeptical about their use when the United States invaded Iraq in March 2003. At that time the robot force consisted mostly of prototype drones. By 2010, however, the military was fielding more than fifty-three hundred drones and more than twelve thousand ground robots. According to Alan S. Brown, associate editor of *Mechanical Engineering—CIME*, "The military has embraced [robots] as a way to reduce risk to soldiers, gather intelligence, and strike stealthily at remote enemies." In fact, many claim that successful drone strikes have effectively disrupted Al Qaeda's leaders hiding near the Afghanistan-Pakistan border.

Nevertheless, even General Mattis expresses concern over what he sees as a potential moral hazard. "From a Marine's point of view, we cannot lose our honor by failing to put our own skin on the line to protect the realm." Thus, in the eyes of some, one of the risks of robot warfare is that soldiers become too disconnected from the field of battle. According to Brown, some reports reveal that drone pilots suffer from higher rates of post-traumatic stress disorder than other soldiers do. "Perhaps this 'disconnect' is part of the reason: It may be harder for a soldier to justify killing when his or her life is not at risk," he opines. Drone pilots may work with people they have never met to direct strikes at an enemy they only see on a video monitor while working out of a trailer on a military base in Nevada. "Those same monitors, however, may show the carnage they inflict, from the wounded writhing on the ground after an attack to families burning in buildings engulfed in flames. After a shift, these same pilots drive home and sit around the dinner table helping their children with homework," notes Brown.

Other analysts add that the growing military use of robots will change the required skills of future soldiers. For example, to become an F-15 fighter pilot takes years of training; to become a drone pilot takes mere months. According to Brown, one of the US Army's top drone pilots was a nineteen-year-old high school dropout who was a particularly adept video gamer. According to director of the 21st-Century Defense Initiative and a Brookings Institution researcher, Peter Singer, one source interviewed for his book on robot warfare, *Wired for War*, claimed that "having a strong bladder and a big butt may turn out to be more useful physical attributes than being able to do 100 pushups." This, for some, is an unsettling picture, particularly for a military culture that is slow to accept change.

Policy makers already struggle with the challenges posed by the use of robotic technology in armed conflict. Whether the increased military use of robots has greater benefits or risks remains hotly contested. Indeed, the authors in the following chapter present their views on related controversies surrounding the question, What role should robotic technology play in war? Although the military establishment now sees robot-based warfare as a great asset, the risks remain. According to *Ethical Spectacle* blogger Thomas G. Vincent, "It's important that we not fall into the trap of thinking that just because our slingshot has a greater range than the other guy's, we are morally justified in using it in every case. Military superiority brings with it a moral responsibility not to use the superior weapons we possess merely because we possess them."

"Robots have become a critical security and intelligence component of 21st century warfare."

Robotic Technology Is a Critical Component of Twenty-First-Century Warfare

Joseph W. Dyer

The United States should continue its leadership in the development of battlefield robots in the twenty-first century, claims Joseph W. Dyer in the following viewpoint. Unmanned robotic vehicles can conduct surveillance and reconnaissance, and, moreover, Dyer argues, unmanned robots can perform dangerous bomb disposal missions and clear routes for military convoys. Indeed, he reasons, robots make the battlefield more survivable. As robots become more autonomous, Dyer asserts, they can also reduce the number of soldiers needed and allow troops to fight from greater distances. Dyer, chief strategy officer at iRobot Corporation and chair of NASA's Aerospace Safety Advisory Panel, has served as a US Navy commander.

As you read, consider the following questions:

1. According to Dyer, in addition to the battlefield, in what other environments are robots performing?

Joseph W. Dyer, "Why the United States Must Win the Robotics Race," Nextgov.com, April 11, 2012. Reproduced by permission.

2. What purpose does retro-traverse functionality serve, in the author's view?

3. In Dyer's opinion, what is the dilemma facing military planners?

Robots have become a critical security and intelligence component of 21st century warfare. As a result of their proven success in combat, the types of missions that robots perform are rapidly expanding on and off the battlefield. This proliferation of practical robots highlights the leadership position of the United States in the global robotics industry and the importance of maintaining it.

Indeed, robotics is one of the two most promising areas of scientific innovation and economic growth in America right now. (Biogenetics is the other.) In the not-so-distant past, the United States enjoyed great economic and technological success with automobiles, aviation, agriculture and information technology. In the near future, robotics has the same potential to be an economic engine that carries the nation forward, providing a foundation for significant enhancements and employment opportunities in defense, research and other critical sectors.

Building on Past Successes

Twenty years ago, robots were mostly an idea. Today, they are performing all kinds of tasks in various environments.

The Defense Department's successful use of robots is a perfect example. Unmanned ground, air and underwater vehicles provide situational awareness and perform bomb disposal, surveillance and reconnaissance, oceanographic research and other missions for armed forces around the world.

The impact isn't just on the battlefield, as robots also are performing tasks in millions of homes, including vacuuming carpets, washing floors and cleaning gutters. Advancements in wireless connectivity, computational horsepower, artificial intelligence, sensors and power efficiency are making new robotic functionality a reality for less cost than ever before. The promise of practical robots is no longer just a promise; the robots are here now and there are going to be many more of them soon.

Preparing for the Future

Today, military robots are largely controlled remotely from a distance and always require a human in the decision-making loop. They are an extension of the soldier and provide a virtual presence, but they require constant operator involvement and heads-down operation [i.e., someone has to be paying attention to what the robots are doing].

As a result, robots will become more valuable as they become more autonomous. Autonomy will reduce bandwidth and personnel requirements. It's also going to break the ratio of one operator to one robot; in the future, one operator will control a dozen robots.

Some simple, limited autonomous capabilities are starting to leave the lab and will make their way into [the] theater [of war] soon. For example, with retro-traverse functionality, when a robot loses communications it retraces its approach path until communications are restored. Retro-traverse eliminates the need for a soldier to go down range and retrieve a disabled robot, which defeats the whole point of using a robot in the first place. Similarly, self-righting technology enables a robot that has been flipped over to automatically right itself and continue the mission without operator intervention, tremendously reducing the operator's overhead and increasing their situational awareness.

Autonomous technology will profoundly affect tactics and doctrine in the future, too. Instead of using a joystick to control a robot, an operator will use his or her voice and hand gestures to direct robots performing as part of a combat team. With advanced autonomy, multiple robots functioning as wingmen and teammates will significantly reduce costs and demands on personnel. At that point, robots will be true force multipliers capable of performing a variety of tasks and coordinated missions, such as collaborative target engagement using unmanned ground and aerial vehicles.

Facing Global Competition

Right now, on the battlefields in Afghanistan, thousands of life-saving military robots are deployed with troops. It's the beginning of a shift to squads with more robots and fewer soldiers. The robots go in first, providing situational awareness for troops from safe standoff distances while inspecting IEDs [improvised explosive devices], clearing convoy routes and performing other dangerous missions.

Although the United States is leading the world in robotics, global competition is picking up. Plenty of other nations— Israel, South Korea, China and Germany, to name a few—also see the incredible potential in robotics. South Korea already has a national industrial strategy for robotics; the United States doesn't at this point. With so much at stake, we need to ensure the United States stays on top.

Of course, competition for resources is always an issue and even more so in a tightening defense market. The dilemma facing military planners is whether budget dollars are spent on ships, tanks, airplanes and the weapons of the past or on unmanned systems and other emerging technologies of the future. It's a tough transition. And it raises another difficult question: what do we do in the interim?

Learning the Lesson

One thing's for sure: we need to learn from the lessons of the last 10 years, particularly with regard to irregular warfare and the cheap, simple asymmetric attacks that have profoundly restricted freedom of action and cost our troops dearly, including the proliferation of IEDs.

A new strategy is emerging. Future conflicts likely will be fought with more special operations troops from greater standoff distances with better situational awareness and better coordination. Robots will be smaller and lighter and they'll perform reconnaissance, clear buildings and conduct raids and other dangerous missions for the infantry and special operations forces, not just for bomb-disposal teams.

With the addition of more robots, the future battlefield generally will be more survivable. In the future, soldiers will be able to leverage intelligent unmanned systems even more so than they do today (and we already do a lot today with satellite feeds, tactical reconnaissance, standoff weapons systems, air strikes and more). Ultimately, unmanned systems will work together collaboratively on the land, in the air and under water to provide enhanced situational awareness and perform coordinated missions.

For national defense and economic growth, the United States must maintain its leadership position in robotics—with what we know today, what we see coming tomorrow and what we don't know will be coming in the distant future.

| "*[Drones are] the most effective and precise tool in our counterterrorism arsenal.*"

Unmanned Aerial Vehicles Effectively Fight Terrorism

Charles G. Kels

Unmanned aerial vehicles, also known as drones, are an effective tool in the fight against terrorism, maintains Charles G. Kels in the following viewpoint. Using drones to target terrorists does not violate international law—the laws of war allow nations to defend themselves when terrorists hide in sovereign states, he asserts. Moreover, Kels claims, the law enforcement model, in which police officers use force only as a last resort, does not apply to soldiers. When nations are either unwilling or unable to pursue terrorists hiding within their borders, drone strikes are an efficient and legal alternative, he reasons. Kels, a major in the US Air Force Reserve, is a Department of Homeland Security attorney.

As you read, consider the following questions:

1. According to Kels, how have human rights lawyers become modern-day Luddites?

2. What historical examples does the author provide to support his claim that states may pursue nonstate actors within other countries?

3. In Kels's opinion, what would be the impact of holding a drone operator to the same standards as a metro police officer?

Human rights lawyers have become modern-day Luddites [those who fear or reject technological progress]. Against all evidence that drone strikes offer unparalleled precision and minimize the loss of life, they insist that utopia would be restored if only we could return to the conventional artillery barrage.

Such distaste for innovation disregards the history of warfare, which is marked by an unending quest to engage the enemy beyond the range of his weaponry. It also misconstrues the legal underpinnings of the fight against al Qaeda.

The hallmark of transnational terrorist networks is seeking safe havens under the umbrella of weak or sympathetic governments, and then using that territory as a launching ground to imperil the citizens of other states. This behavior challenges the paradigm of interstate conflicts and civil wars—the twin frameworks upon which the international laws of war are built.

Breaching Sovereignty in Self-Defense

Nations possess an inherent right of self-defense, as recognized by Article 51 of the United Nations Charter. Transnational terrorists throw a wrench into this scheme because exercising self-defense against their attacks necessarily involves breaching the sovereignty of the state that is harboring them, whether by virtue of its hapless condition or complicity.

The answer is not, as some commentators would have it, for accountable nations either to throw up their hands in despair or to launch a full-scale invasion. The former would be derelict, the latter disproportionate.

Instead, the United States reasonably invokes a corollary of the self-defense principle, which posits that one state may unilaterally employ force against non-state actors within another country that is either "unwilling or unable" to do so itself. This position rests upon the presumption that, as one commentator puts it, "respect for sovereignty is subject to the responsibility of sovereignty."

This doctrine did not arise with the advent of armed drones, and has deeper roots than critics of U.S. counterterrorism efforts care to admit. In a 1989 speech, the State Department's legal adviser affirmed "the legality of a nation attacking a terrorist base from which attacks on its citizens are being launched, if the host country is either unwilling or unable to stop the terrorists from using its territory for that purpose."

Going back much further, the British felt justified in 1837 to enter U.S. territory and set fire to the SS *Caroline*, which had been utilized by American sympathizers to aid Canadian rebels in their fight against the crown. Indeed, St. Augustine wrote in the early 5th century that a just war could be waged against a nation that "has neglected to punish a wrong committed by its citizens."

When aggrieved nations pursue terrorists into states that are either "unwilling or unable" to confront them, they are obliged to conduct such operations in accordance with the standards applicable to military force. This law of armed conflict, although a sacred and time-tested tool for alleviating some of war's worst horrors, is necessarily more permissive than the rules governing everyday activities.

Soldiers Are Not Police Officers

In a nutshell, the law requires armed forces to distinguish between military and civilian targets and only attack the former,

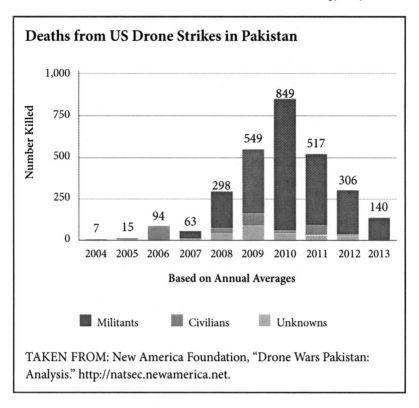

Deaths from US Drone Strikes in Pakistan

Based on Annual Averages

Militants — Civilians — Unknowns

TAKEN FROM: New America Foundation, "Drone Wars Pakistan: Analysis." http://natsec.newamerica.net.

while balancing the unintended consequences to the latter (collateral damage) against the legitimate value of the mission. Thus, the rules for soldiers differ substantially from police officers, for whom lethal force is a last resort and apprehension remains the overarching goal.

Human rights advocates, in turn, fret that an inevitable "war-creep" in the pursuit of terrorists will convert the entire world into a combat zone. They insist upon a "legal geography of war," whereby states must apply a law enforcement (rather than armed conflict) model to any hostilities conducted outside of universally recognized "hot battlefields" like Afghanistan.

This solution is, of course, untenable to threatened nations, who refuse to countenance safe havens for roving terrorist bands. It is also unworkable because police authority assumes control on the ground and establishing such control would first demand a wide-ranging military assault—along with ensuing casualties on both sides.

Holding a drone operator, fighter pilot or sailor directing ordnance at an overseas terrorist hideout to the same detain-first, shoot-last standards as a Metro police officer would negate the very purpose of the weapons system, which is precisely the goal of some activists. Sadly, such technophobia cloaked in the language of human rights law would actually cost more lives by neutering the most effective and precise tool in our counterterrorism arsenal.

Drones, by virtue of their geographic reach, enable advanced states to take the fight to transnational terrorists as never before. Their proper use does not violate international law. That distinction belongs to the transnational terrorists themselves.

"If [drones] are the 'only game in town in terms of confronting or trying to disrupt Al Qaeda leadership' then we are truly in failure mode."

Unmanned Aerial Vehicles Alone Are Inadequate to Fight Terrorism

Paul Sullivan

In the following viewpoint, Paul Sullivan argues that drones alone are an ineffective strategy to fight terrorism. The backlash against the killing of women and children in fact threatens the war on terror, he reasons. The better strategy is to encourage the people to oppose terrorists in nations where they hide, Sullivan asserts. In truth, the best way to promote opposition to terrorists in these nations is to help the people live better lives, he maintains. Although drones have killed some terrorists, the United States should not consider these strikes a long-term success, Sullivan concludes. Sullivan is a professor of economics at National Defense University in Washington, DC.

Paul Sullivan, "Are Drone Strikes the Only Game in Town?," *National Journal*, January 11, 2010. Reproduced by permission.

As you read, consider the following questions:

1. What does Sullivan claim is part of the explanation for the nonterrorist deaths that some drone attacks have caused?

2. According to the author, why have many nations turned on the Israelis?

3. Who does the author claim might be the most powerful peacemakers around?

If predators [a type of drone aircraft] are the "only game in town in terms of confronting or trying to disrupt Al Qaeda leadership" then we are truly in failure mode. Such high velocity technological solutions should be just one of the many arrows in the complex quiver we need.

Al Qaeda often lives in the shadows. It also often tries to communicate via non-electronic and somewhat traditional means. Also, the drones are controlled sometimes from long distances and at high altitudes, and without real time information backing them up constantly. This may be part of the explanation for the non-terrorist deaths that some of the drone attacks have caused.

We most definitely need to consider the public backlash. Wars are not won and lost with just technologies and speedy devices. They are won with public support and a more stabilized and stabilizing social psychology on the ground. The most important part of any war is developing the peace that can happen after it. Killing women, children, old persons and other innocents in the pursuit of extremists may likely cause greater recruitment into the violent extremist groups. Then what are the end results? Is this a victory? No. Public support has often been less after such attacks than before. Clearly something is wrong with this approach.

The Failed Israeli Strategy

The Israeli experience of counterinsurgency and counterterrorism is not a success story. Anyone who thinks it has been should visit Gaza.

How could anyone consider the Israeli strategy of the attacks on Gaza winning ones? Gaza is a ticking time bomb like no other the Israelis have faced. The Egyptians also have to deal with this ticking time bomb. Gaza is more of a threat to Egypt now than ever before. The situation in Gaza is also building up tensions in the streets and coffee houses, and extremist meeting rooms, in many other Arab and Muslim countries. [Militant organization] Hamas and the mafias run Gaza.

The West Bank is in more of a boil than in many times in the past. Many of the Arab states that once had efforts to help develop warming relations with the Israelis have backed off. Many in the EU [European Union] and elsewhere have turned on them. Frankly, Israel may be more insecure now than at any time since its founding in 1948 even though it has lots of high-tech weapons. Weapons are not sufficient to bring security.

Many in Israel understand the complexities that they face in the Palestinian Territories. Some of their best strategists see that the solutions to their security problems are often elusive, but that they will necessarily involve much more than technologies such as drones. A full spectrum policy that includes political, diplomatic, informational, economic and other strategies will be needed. Drones do not get at the root causes of the Israeli-Arab conflict and they may likely make it much worse.

A One-Dimensional Solution

The drones have killed a few Al Qaeda, Taliban and others. In the murky world of terror groups that are constantly in metamorphosis these directed drone attacks should not be expected to be long term or even medium term wins. Leaders can be replaced. Foot soldiers can be even more easily replaced. These are short term wins. Other strategies and methods need to be used to shore up even these short term wins. Again, a full spectrum approach is needed. One-dimensional solutions are destined to failure.

Counter terrorism is the ultimate in asymmetric warfare. That also means that what one side might consider a major victory the other side might just see as a relatively small to medium-sized annoyance. Just because we are using speedy drones does not mean we are no longer a lumbering and quite obviously big target. Just because we are using drones does not mean that Al Qaeda and others cannot fairly quickly adjust to that threat through some sort of strategic metamorphosis, which is more easily done by small groups than by large.

That is an interesting point about the extrajudicial killings. You don't have to think too hard to see how such killings without trials by high-tech gadgets may negatively affect the impressions the local populations and others may have about the rule of law as applied by the United States. This is way beyond the intellectual exercise of arguing about just actions in war. These actions have some serious and strategically important subsidiary implications. Surely lethality is needed in some circumstances. This is war. But there are ripple effects that need to be considered to understand the true costs and benefits of such actions.

Powerful Peacemakers

The only way to win against the terrorists is by having the people in the areas in regions where the terrorists are found to completely turn against them. Our best allies could be the local populations. The best weapon of war against the terrorists is the weapon of the power of positive culture in these areas and regions. This war cannot be won without the people of the Muslim world behind us. This will not happen if we continue to antagonize, alienate and frighten them.

Sure we can hear the praises from the local contractors who thank us for our efforts, etc, but these are not the most important parts of the populations that need to see, and see clearly, that the violent extremists are a common enemy that needs to be weakened severely, disrupted, and confronted.

What is the best way to confront and disrupt the violent extremists? The violent extremists, such as the Taliban, profess a perverted and heretical version of "Islam". The truth is a powerful weapon. This war is, in part, an ideological one and interpretive one that is internal to the Muslim world. The intellectual and spiritual warriors of truth in the Muslim world may be the most powerful peacemakers around.

However, as this war grinds on, the moderates are losing ground to the extremists. If this continues much more we could be all truly in much more danger and the body bag count will go way up.

We need to get beyond football analogies and start thinking about other forms of warfare, peace building and peace making.

We need to develop better relations with the people of the regions in which this war is being fought. Drones don't do that. Helping them live better lives and helping to develop hope for a better world does. None of that is easy. None of that is immediate. The policies and strategies will need to be multidimensional and multi-decade. Anyone who is looking for a quick fix with drones is destined to be sorely disappointed—and wrong.

Unless we look at the full spectrum, cultural, economic, political, diplomatic, informational approach even the concept of winning is elusive. Ever wonder why? Because winning is impossible without the Muslim world winning its own battles against poverty, unemployment, extremism, perverted ideologies, and more. We can see them as 1.5 billion potential allies and partners in the common struggles and hopes for a better, more peaceful and prosperous world or—we can lose.

| "It is imperative that we create international legislation . . . for autonomous robots at war."

International Laws Governing Autonomous Military Robots Are Necessary

Noel Sharkey

Nations worldwide are actively pursuing autonomous robot soldiers, claims Noel Sharkey in the following viewpoint. Although robots are less costly, allowing machines to make the decision to take a human life is dangerous, he maintains. In fact, Sharkey suggests, tests so far show that robot soldiers cannot easily discriminate between combatants and civilians, let alone make complex ethical decisions. Since international laws currently treat robots as weapons and not soldiers, nations must agree to new laws governing autonomous robots at war, he reasons. Sharkey is professor of artificial intelligence and robotics at the University of Sheffield in South Yorkshire, England.

As you read, consider the following questions:

1. According to Sharkey, what has the US Congress stated as its 2015 goal regarding combat vehicles?

Noel Sharkey, "Robot Wars Are a Reality," *The Guardian* (UK), August 17, 2007. Reproduced by permission.

2. What are the war-fighting benefits of autonomous vehicles, in the author's view?

3. In the author's opinion, what is a possible motive for a US Army project to equip robot soldiers with a conscience?

The deployment of the first armed battlefield robots in Iraq is the latest step on a dangerous path—we are sleepwalking into a brave new world where robots decide who, where and when to kill. Already, South Korea and Israel are deploying armed robot border guards and China, Singapore and the UK [United Kingdom] are among those making increasing use of military robots. The biggest player yet is the US: robots are integral to its $230bn future combat systems project, a massive plan to develop unmanned vehicles that can strike from the air, under the sea and on land. Congress has set a goal of having one-third of ground combat vehicles unmanned by 2015. Over 4,000 robots are serving in Iraq at present, others in Afghanistan. And now they are armed. Most robots currently in combat are extensions of human fighters who control the application of lethal force. When a semi-autonomous MQ-1 Predator self-navigated above a car full of al-Qaida suspects in 2002, the decision to vaporise them with Hellfire missiles was made by pilots 7,000 miles away. Predators and the more deadly Reaper robot attack planes have flown many missions since then with inevitable civilian deaths, yet working with remote-controlled or semi-autonomous machines carries only the same ethical responsibilities as a traditional air strike.

A Dangerous New Territory

But fully autonomous robots that make their own decisions about lethality are high on the US military agenda. The US National Research Council advises "aggressively exploiting the considerable warfighting benefits offered by autonomous vehicles". They are cheap to manufacture, require less personnel and, according to the navy, perform better in complex missions. One battlefield soldier could start a large-scale robot attack in the air and on the ground.

This is dangerous new territory for warfare, yet there are no new ethical codes or guidelines in place. I have worked in artificial intelligence for decades, and the idea of a robot making decisions about human termination is terrifying. Policymakers seem to have an understanding of AI that lies in the realms of science fiction and myth. A recent US navy document suggests that the critical issue is for autonomous systems to be able to identify the legality of targets. Then their answer to the ethical problems is simply, "Let men target men" and "Let machines target other machines". In reality, a robot could not pinpoint a weapon without pinpointing the person using it or even discriminate between weapons and non-weapons. I can imagine a little girl being zapped because she points her ice cream at a robot to share. Or a robot could be tricked into killing innocent civilians.

Delegating Responsibility for Fatal Errors

In attempting to allay political opposition, the US army is funding a project to equip robot soldiers with a conscience to give them the ability to make ethical decisions. But machines could not discriminate reliably between buses carrying enemy soldiers or schoolchildren, let alone be ethical. It smells like a move to delegate the responsibility for fatal errors on to non-sentient weapons.

Human soldiers have legal protocols such as the Geneva conventions to guide them. Autonomous robots are only covered by the laws of armed conflict that deal with standard weapons. But autonomous robots are not like other weapons. We are going to give decisions on human fatality to machines that are not bright enough to be called stupid. With prices falling and technology becoming easier, we may soon see a robot arms race that will be difficult to stop.

It is imperative that we create international legislation and a code of ethics for autonomous robots at war before it is too late.

"Autonomous armed robotic platforms may ... better adhere to the Laws of War than most soldiers possibly can."

Ethical Robots in Warfare

Ronald C. Arkin

In the following viewpoint, Ronald C. Arkin maintains that robots can behave more humanely and ethically on the battlefield than human soldiers can. Unlike humans, who often struggle with decision making under the stress of war, autonomous robots do not have to contend with self-preservation, he claims. Moreover, Arkin asserts, developers can program robots with sensors that make them better than humans at making battlefield observations. Nevertheless, he concedes, robotic scientists must ensure that the use of robotic technology in war remains ethical. Arkin, a professor and director of the Mobile Robot Laboratory at the Georgia Institute of Technology, is author of Governing Lethal Behavior in Autonomous Robots.

As you read, consider the following questions:

1. In Arkin's view, what is forcing autonomy further toward the point of robots making that final decision to take human life in war?

Arkin, R.C. 2009. "Ethical Robots in Warfare," *IEEE Technology and Society Magazine,* vol. 28, no. 1, Spring 2009, pp. 30–33. Reproduced with permission.

2. According to the author, what contributed to the downing of an Iranian airliner by the USS *Vincennes* in 1988?

3. What does Arkin claim are some of the operational benefits of autonomous robotic systems?

R obotic system capabilities have advanced dramatically over the last several decades. We now have artificially intelligent systems and robots that are stronger than humans, that can venture places where people cannot go (such as Mars), that are smarter than people in certain cases (e.g., in chess), and so on. We are no longer truly surprised when machine artifacts outperform humans in new domains.

But the outperformance of humans by artificially intelligent systems may still come as a surprise to some. It is a thesis of my ongoing research for the U.S. Army that robots not only can be better than soldiers in conducting warfare in certain circumstances, but they also can be more humane in the battlefield than humans.

Making Decisions in the Heat of Combat

Why should this surprise us? Do we believe that human warfighters exhibit the best of humanity in battlefield situations? There is strong evidence to the contrary, and we have developed Laws of War to criminalize those people who behave outside of acceptable international norms. Despite these regulations, they are often cast aside in the heat of combat, for reasons such as vengeance, anger, frustration, and the desire for victory at any cost.

Robots already have the ability to carry weapons and use lethal force under the direction of a human operator. Multiple unmanned robotic systems are already being developed or are in use that employ lethal force, such as the Armed Robotic Vehicle (ARV), a component of the Future Combat System (FCS); Predator and Reaper unmanned aerial vehicles (UAVs) equipped with Hellfire missiles, which have already been used in combat but under direct human supervision; and the development of an armed platform for use in the Korean Demilitarized Zone, to name only a few. These and other systems are not fully autonomous in this sense: they do not currently make decisions on their own about when, or not, to engage a target. But the pressure of an increasing battlefield tempo is forcing autonomy further and further towards the point of robots making that final, lethal decision. The time available to make the decision to shoot or not to shoot is becoming too short for remote humans to make intelligent, informed decisions in many situations that arise in modern warfare. As that time dwindles, robots will likely be given more authority to make lethal decisions on their own.

Commercially available robots already have had emotions engineered into them; e.g., the robot dog AIBO, so researchers, at least to some extent, have an understanding of what affect contributes to intelligent interaction with humans. It is my contention that robots can be built that do not exhibit fear, anger, frustration, or revenge, and that ultimately (and the key word here is ultimately) behave in a more humane manner than even human beings in these harsh circumstances and severe duress. People have not evolved to function in these conditions, but robots can be engineered to function well in them.

Robot Adherence to Laws of War

In my book entitled *Governing Lethal Behavior in Autonomous Robots*, I make the case that autonomous armed robotic platforms may ultimately reduce noncombatant casualties and other forms of collateral damage by their ability to better adhere to the Laws of War than most soldiers possibly can. Some of the material that follows is drawn directly from this book. Many of my colleagues . . . argue against this thesis and bring up many significant issues that must be resolved prior to such a deployment. To summarize both sides of these arguments, first, the reasons why ethical autonomy can succeed include the following:

1. The ability to act conservatively: Robots do not need to protect themselves in cases of low certainty of target identification. Autonomous armed robotic vehicles do not need to have self-preservation as a foremost drive, if at all. They can be used in a self-sacrificing manner if needed and appropriate, without reservation by a commanding officer.

2. The eventual development and use of a broad range of robotic sensors better equipped for battlefield observations than human sensory abilities.

3. Robots can be designed without emotions that cloud their judgment or result in anger and frustration with ongoing battlefield events. In addition, "Fear and hysteria are always latent in combat, often real, and they press us toward fearful measures and criminal behavior." Autonomous agents need not suffer similarly.

4. Avoidance of the human psychological problem of "scenario fulfillment" is possible, a factor believed partly contributing to the downing of an Iranian Airliner by the USS *Vincennes* in 1988. This phenomena leads to distortion or neglect of contradictory information in stressful situations, where humans use new incoming information in ways that fit only their pre-existing belief patterns, a form of premature cognitive closure. Robots need not be vulnerable to such patterns of behavior.

5. Robots can integrate more information from more sources far more quickly before responding with lethal force than a human can in real-time. This information and data can arise from multiple remote sensors and intelligence (including human) sources, as part of the

Army's network-centric warfare concept and the concurrent development of the Global Information Grid. "Military systems (including weapons) now on the horizon will be too fast, too small, too numerous, and will create an environment too complex for humans to direct".

6. When working on a team of combined human soldiers and autonomous systems as an organic asset, robots have the potential capability of independently and objectively monitoring ethical behavior in the battlefield by all parties and reporting infractions that might be observed. This presence alone might possibly lead to a reduction in human ethical infractions.

Additional Battlefield Robot Benefits

Aside from these ethical considerations, autonomous robotic systems offer numerous potential operational benefits to the military: faster, cheaper, better mission accomplishment; longer range, greater persistence, longer endurance, higher precision; faster target engagement; and immunity to chemical and biological weapons, among other benefits. All of these can enhance mission effectiveness and serve as drivers for the ongoing deployment of these systems.

But this new research focuses on enhancing ethical benefits by using these systems, ideally without eroding mission performance when compared to human warfighters.

The Arguments Against Use of Wartime Robots

The counterarguments against the use of lethal autonomous systems are numerous as well:

- Establishing responsibility—who's to blame if things go wrong with an autonomous robot?

- The threshold of entry into warfare may be lowered as we will now be risking machines and fewer human sol-

Robots and the Laws of War

In the not-too-distant future, relatively autonomous robots may be capable of conducting warfare in a way that matches or exceeds the traditional *jus in bello* [right in war] morality of a human soldier. With a properly programmed slave morality [in which the robot's goals are determined by humans], a robot can ensure it will not violate the LOW [laws of war] or ROE [rules of engagement], and it can even become a superior peacekeeper after official hostilities have ceased. And of course, having robots fight for us promises to dramatically reduce casualties on our side and may become a fearsome enough weapon that eventually war will cease to be a desirable option by nation-states as a means of resolving their differences. Once such robots exist and have been properly trained through simulations, there will be little moral justification to keep them sidelined: if war is to be fought, we will have good moral reason to have the robots do the fighting for us.

Patrick Lin, George Bekey, and Keith Abney,
"Autonomous Military Robotics: Risk, Ethics, and Design",
white paper for the US Navy, December 20, 2008.

diers—this could violate the Jus ad Bellum ["right to war"] conditions of just warfare.

- The possibility of unilateral risk-free warfare, which could be viewed as potentially unjust.

- It simply can't be done right—it's just too hard for machines to discriminate targets.

- The effect on military squad cohesion and its impact on the fighting force—human warfighters may not accept ethical robots monitoring their performance.

- Robots running amok—the classic science fiction nightmare.

- A robot refusing an order—the question of whether ultimate authority should vest in humans.

- The issues of overrides placed in the hands of immoral, irresponsible, or reckless individuals.

- The co-opting of an ethical robot research effort by the military to serve to justify other political agendas.

- The difficulty in winning the hearts and minds of the civilians affected by warfare if robots are allowed to kill.

- Proliferation of the technology to other nations and terrorists. . . .

I am confident that these contrarian issues are raised in more detail . . . by the other authors . . . and I will not elaborate on them here. Some are more easily dismissed than others, some are not unique to autonomous robot battlefield technology, some can be addressed by recognizing that we're dealing with bounded morality for very narrow tactical situations and are not replacing a human solider one-for-one, and some can be addressed by suitable system design which may be long range but nonetheless feasible. Space, however, prevents a full and fair treatment of these concerns here. The goal of my research on ethical autonomous systems capable of lethal action is to provide robots with an ethical code that has been already established by humanity as encoded in the Laws of War and the Rules of Engagement. Robots must be constrained to adhere to the same laws as humans or they should not be permitted on the battlefield. This further implies that they must have the right to refuse an order which is determined to be unethical, and that they possess the ability to monitor and report on the ethical behavior of other military personnel as required.

Examining Ethical Responsibilities

I think of myself as a responsible scientist who has spent decades working on military applications of robotics. I think the following questions are crucial:

> Is it not our responsibility as scientists to look for effective ways to reduce human inhumanity to other people through technology? And if such inhumanity occurs during warfare, what can be done?

It is my belief that research in *ethical* military robotics can and should be applied towards achieving this end. But how can this happen? Where does humanity fit on the battlefield? Extrapolating these questions further, we ask:

Should soldiers be robots? Isn't that largely what they are trained to be?

Should robots be soldiers? Could they be more humane than humans?

One lesson I have learned along the way is that roboticists should not run from the difficult ethical issues surrounding the use of their intellectual property that is or will be applied to warfare, whether or not they directly participate. Wars unfortunately will continue and derivative technology from these ideas will be used. If your robotics research is of significance and it is published openly, it will be put to use in military systems by someone, somewhere, someday. Researchers are not immune from contributing to military applications by simply not accepting funds from the U.S. Department of Defense [DOD]. To ensure proper usage of this technology, proactive management by all parties concerned is necessary. Complete relinquishment of robotics research as proposed by Bill Joy is the only alternative, but I do not personally favor that strategy.

I remain active in my research for the U.S. DOD in battlefield applications of robotics for both the U.S. Army and Navy regarding the deployment of teams of robots, but it remains a personal goal that these systems and other related military research products will ultimately be ethically restrained by technological methods so as to abide by the internationally agreed upon Laws of War. I also hope that this research will spur others into not only considering this problem, but to help ensure that warfare is conducted justly, even with the advent of autonomous robots if international societies so deem it fit, and that those who step beyond those ethical bounds, whoever they may be, are successfully prosecuted for their war crimes. It is my conviction that as these weaponized autonomous systems appear on the battlefield, they should help to ensure that humanity, proportionality, responsibility, and relative safety, as encoded in the Laws of War, are extended during combat not only to friendly forces, but equally to noncombatants and those who are otherwise hors de combat [outside the fight], with the goal being a reduction in the loss of life of civilians and all other forms of collateral damage.

> *"The military isn't ready for the next generation of mechanized soldiers. Letting a robot enter an enclosed space with a weapon, and giving it the ability to defend itself, could be too far of a leap for the military community to accept."*

The US Military Remains Reluctant to Accept Autonomous Robot Soldiers

Stew Magnuson

Although robots might keep soldiers from harm, those developing robot soldiers must be careful when introducing this technology to military decision makers, claims Stew Magnuson in the following viewpoint. Indeed, robot designers recognize the gap between those who develop technology and those who use technology in the field, he reports. Despite the billions invested in autonomous robot research, soldiers are skeptical of allowing a robot to carry weapons, Magnuson maintains. However, he concludes, the success of ordnance-disposal robots is breaking down some walls. Magnuson, a former foreign correspondent, is managing editor of National Defense *magazine.*

Stew Magnuson, "War Machines: For Now, Lethal Robots Not Likely to Run on Auto-Pilot," *National Defense*, vol. 92, no. 652, March 2008, p. 30. Reproduced by permission.

As you read, consider the following questions:

1. According to Magnuson, what can an autonomous reconnaissance robot do?

2. Why are the German Goliath suicide robots of World War II largely forgotten, in the author's view?

3. In the author's opinion, what do a hunting dog and war fighter's associate robot have in common?

Bart Everett, technical director for robots at the Navy's space and naval warfare systems center, acknowledged that the military isn't ready for the next generation of mechanized soldiers.

He is nevertheless overseeing the development of a robot soldier. One that will enter into a building alongside a human companion uses sensors to seek out enemies, then fire lethal or nonlethal weapons to eliminate targets.

He calls the concept the "war fighter's associate" and likens the human-robot relationship to that of a hunter and a bird-dog.

"What we have to do is work with the war fighter and figure out what [he] will accept. . . . If I lay this on him right away, it's going to freak him out," Everett said.

Classic Disconnect

The problem boils down to the classic disconnect between those who work on cutting edge technologies in the lab and the users in the field, he said. The engineers have no idea what the soldier really needs and the conditions he encounters. And the soldiers don't know what technologies are available to them and what they can do.

Everett said the lab is about 10 years ahead of where he expected to be in terms of achieving autonomy for robots.

Autonomy means little or no need for an operator to use a joystick. A reconnaissance robot, for example, can be sent into a bunker without any radio link, and come out with a complete map populated with icons showing the location of people, weapons, or evidence of weapons of mass destruction.

And it may mean allowing that robot to have a weapon to defend itself in case it comes under attack.

That by itself could cause skeptics to shake their heads. Letting a robot enter an enclosed space with a weapon, and giving it the ability to defend itself, could be too far of a leap for the military community to accept, he said.

The Problems with Past Robots

As Everett sees it, the way robots are controlled has not evolved since World War II [1939–1945].

The fact that there were robots used that long ago in wartime is a surprise to most even those in the industry, he said. The Germans built 8,000 Goliath suicide robots. They were a few feet long, moved on tank-like tracks and were loaded with explosives. They were designed to drive up to bunkers or tanks and then blow up.

One reason that they are largely forgotten today is that they were not very successful, said Everett, who is writing a book on the topic.

They were tele-operated—meaning that they needed a soldier to control the machine through a radio link. These links failed, and therefore, so did the robots.

When the U.S. military invaded Iraq more than six decades later, it arrived with about 170 robots—about 7,800 fewer than the Germans had. And when these radio-controlled machines lost their links, they also failed.

After spending about a billion dollars on robotics research and development funds, Everett said he finds it lamentable that the United States is still using tele-operated robots. Controlling a robot in a battle zone is an engrossing task for the operator, and therefore dangerous. That's why his lab, and others, are intensely working on achieving autonomy.

"The problem we have is the war fighter is just getting used to World War II technology," he added.

Breakthroughs in Autonomous Robots

In the SPAWAR [Space and Naval Warfare Systems Command] laboratories [in San Diego], work continues on some of the leap-ahead concepts that he said the military is not ready to accept.

One of these systems, Robart III, carries a gun and a small rocket launcher. Electronics engineer Brandon Sights gave it a command to "follow" and it kept pace with him through the room and door into the California sunshine.

Sights picked up a rifle and pointed it towards the sea and Robart's weapons did the same.

SPAWAR is not researching how to make the robot walk up and down stairs. There are other laboratories and organizations such as the Defense Advanced Research Projects Agency and its Big Dog project, working on walking robots. At some point, these two technologies—autonomous function and human or animal-like mobility—may be married, he predicted.

Another breakthrough has been in the realm of vision. Everett decided about two years ago [in 2006] that current algorithms—designed to let a robot see and understand what is around it through camera lenses—were too complicated.

When a man walks down the street, his brain is only taking in on a conscious level a small percentage of what he is seeing. The rest is filtered out and pushed down to the subconscious. If something catches his attention, then he will turn his head and focus on that object.

SPAWAR robots were already outfitted with ladars to help them navigate rooms and avoid obstacles. Ladars send out laser pulses to measure distances. The epiphany was to make the ladar the "subconscious." If it picks up an anomaly—an object leaning against a wall—then it can move over to the target, switch on the vision, and decide what it is by comparing the shape of the object to those stored in its memory. Is it shaped like a rifle? If it is a common weapon like an AK-47 [assault rifle], it should be able to identify it.

Earlier experiments were making robots walk into a room, then try to identify everything within its field of view. They became overloaded quickly.

"In the event it can't be identified, take a picture of it, and ID it later," Everett said.

The Benefits of Robot-Human Teams

This realization was one of the breakthroughs that led to SPAWAR being ahead of where it expected to be in terms of autonomy, he said.

"Because of the change in our approach, we've made a lot faster progress."

Just as a hunting dog picks up on his master's non-verbal cues, the war fighter's associate robots are doing the same, Everett said.

Like dogs, "robots can do some things humans can't and vice versa."

If put together as a team, the robot can be sent ahead to do missions that keeps the soldier out of harm's way.

Like a dog's ears and nose, a robot's sensors are superior to a human's.

"We're setting the bar pretty high if we want the robot to be as perceptive as a [dog], Everett admitted. But there is one way to cheat.

Programs such as the Army's land warrior integrated modular fighting system, which envisions a sensor-embedded uniform that can monitor a soldier's vital signs, can be linked . . . just as the weapon's status has already been tied to Robart. The robot could then pick up on the same non-verbal cues that dogs can read.

Military Elites Are Often Challenged by New Tech

Existing military elites are often challenged by new technologies: When a 19-year-old enlisted Army drone pilot can kill more enemy combatants and save more American lives in one day than an Air Force F-15 pilot, the latter is going to look at that drone pilot in much the same way the armored knights must have looked at peasants with guns.

Military History, *"P.W. Singer: The Rise of Robotic Warfare,"* March 2010.

"No one is controlling it, no one is talking to it, and yet it's right there with the [soldier] doing what it is supposed to be doing," Everett said. "We have so many elements of that working right now, it's spooky."

The Leap to Arming Robots

However, an armed robot entering close quarters with humans is another big leap in terms of acceptance. Fratricide is the first problem that comes to mind.

Everett has installed five different sensors into the robot so it can keep track of friendly forces.

These technologies can be married to modern day fire control systems, which are highly accurate. Such systems can already track and destroy a target from a moving Apache helicopter at distances measured in miles. Scaling those capabilities down to meters does not pose a problem, he said.

An armed robot with body armor could walk into an ambush, "coolly find targets, and prioritize them, without getting scared, without making a mistake." He said the robots may actually have fewer friendly fire incidents than their human counterparts.

"In a constricted environment you don't want to go one on one with a computer controlled weapon system. You're not going to win that one. The robot is going to get you before you get it. He's got sensors that can see in the dark, see through smoke, whatever."

Whether the military will embrace such a system is unknown. Meanwhile, laboratories and programs such as his continue to move in that direction.

Breaking Barriers

Barriers in "acceptance" continue to be broken, he said. The first was robots themselves and the belief that they could not perform as well as humans. The highly successful explosive-ordnance-disposal robots, although tele-operated, broke that wall down, he asserted.

Next came armed robots. Some said it would never happen. But last summer [2007], the special weapons observation remote reconnaissance (SWORDS) armed robot entered combat toting a M249 light machine gun. Again, Everett dismissively noted that humans control the guns and platform through radio frequencies. But nonetheless, it was another barrier broken.

Now, there are already inquiries as to whether these robots can be outfitted with nonlethal weapons so they can independently protect themselves from tampering, he said.

This summer [2008], the military will see some of the first fully autonomous robots on bases throughout the United States.

The SPAWAR-built mobile detection and assessment response system (MDARS) will patrol domestic installations under a program run by the Army, which has tri-service responsibility for base security.

"There's no human driving this thing. It is all automatic," Everett said.

MDARS will use 360-degree sensors to detect motion for distances of up to 300 meters. Once it spots "purposeful movement"—in other words an object displaying human-like motions—its speaker blares out a warning:

"Intruder Stop! Stop and be identified."

If there is no response, it shoots a swath of pepper balls in front of the intruder. It can track up to six targets at a time.

With the ability to track so many targets at once, then lay down fire, it's not hard to imagine MDARS being converted to some kind of battle-bot with an array of lethal weapons instead of pepper-ball guns.

Everett acknowledged that this could come to pass, although this version of MDARS would not be ready for that. It would not perform well in rough terrain, for example.

Still, outfitting a robot with a nonlethal weapon it is authorized to fire without a human in the loop is another step in the evolution.

The military may decide it never wants an autonomous robot carrying a lethal weapon. "No problem. We just back off to what [they] will accept." Everett said.

"Just make sure you keep getting their feedback and you're not diverging on some spooky laboratory path that nobody wants to go down, and it will work out. If you try to force something on them they're not ready for, it's going to backfire."

Periodical and Internet Sources Bibliography

The following articles have been selected to supplement the diverse views presented in this chapter.

Thomas J. Billitteri	"Drone Warfare," *CQ Researcher*, August 6, 2010.
Andrew Callam	"Drone Wars: Armed Unmanned Aerial Vehicles," *International Affairs Review*, Winter 2010.
David Dortright	"The Prospect of Global Drone Warfare," CNN Wire, October 19, 2011. http://cnnnewssource.com.
The Economist	"Flight of the Drones," October 8, 2011.
T'Jae Gibson	"Improving, Increasing Robotic System Capabilities: Army Collaborates with Industry, Academia to Develop Autonomous Warfare," *Soldiers Magazine*, August 2011.
Ben Hargreaves	"Ethical Dilemma: With the Growing Use of Robotics in Defence, Experts Are Hoping for a New Morality in Warfare," *Professional Engineering*, October 20, 2010.
Patrick Lin	"Robots, Ethics and War," Stanford University Center for Internet and Society blog, December 15, 2010. http://cyberlaw.stanford.edu.
Peter Singer	"The Drone Dilemma," *New York Times Upfront*, May 14, 2012.
Don Troop	"Robots at War: Scholars Debate the Ethical Issues," *Chronicle of Higher Education*, September 10, 2012.

OPPOSING VIEWPOINTS® SERIES

CHAPTER 3

What Ethical, Legal, and Moral Issues Relate to Robotic Technology?

Chapter Preface

"How do you measure value? By the price tag? By the need? By the blood and sweat that goes into making something? Robots do not produce labor value.... There is no mechanical Karl Marx to save them." These lines come from a short play by Don Mitchell titled *Metal Lunch* that portrays the life of the robot laborer as one of danger, monotony, and desperation. Although the robots of the play resemble the humans exploited during early twentieth-century industrialization, unlike humans, Mitchell's robots have no voice—no way to express their suffering. At present, most people view robots as programmed machines, lacking senses or emotions, unable to experience suffering or fear and thus not alive—not human. Indeed, most of the ethical, legal, and moral issues in the robotic technology debate center on fears of how robots of the future will behave among people or whether engineers should develop such robots in the first place. Some researchers, however, express concern over how humans will respond to and behave alongside these future robots and whether robots will need legal protection.

Indeed, some suggest that judicial systems will, at some point in the future, grant civil rights to robots. According to Phil McNally and Sohail Inayatullah, futurists and planners with the Hawaii Judiciary, the response to this possibility is often one of scorn or disbelief. Some fellow futurists claim that such matters pale when measured against concerns about the potential economic, geopolitical, and social problems posed by robots. Despite this scorn, however, McNally and Inayatullah conclude that legal systems will ultimately recognize the rights of robots. This event, they argue, will be historically significant as "such an extension of rights obviously presupposes a future that will be fundamentally different from the present. The granting of rights to robots may promote a new appreciation of the interrelated rights and responsibilities of humans, machines and nature." This event will in their view involve a significant shift in the Western worldview.

How civil rights are defined varies among cultures. The modern Western view of the rights of humans evolved primarily from a convergence of scientific, economic, religious, and social philosophies during the seventeenth and eighteenth centuries. According to Western thought, humanity not only assumes domination over nature but is also entitled to natural rights. This philosophy was ultimately institutionalized into the legal system. For capitalism to flourish, however, a clear division of capital, labor, and resources was necessary. Thus, capital—white men who owned land and/or hereditary titles— would exploit labor—an underclass of workers—and resources, namely, nature. In order to justify this exploitation ideologically, capitalists would have to consider the exploited less than human. "Thus, nature, those in the colonies and the underclass within industrialized nations (women and the proletariat) had to be denied certain rights," assert McNally and Inayatullah. From this, the two futurists generalize that because robotic technology is tied to capitalism, humans will exploit robots because robots are machines—less than human. Indeed, they argue, "humans have defined numerous groups as less than human: slaves, woman, the 'other races,' children, and foreigners. These are the wretched who have been defined as stateless, personless, as suspect, as rightless. This is the present realm of robotic rights." In their view, robots will only gain rights if doing so strengthens capitalism or during a crisis, such as the threat of anarchy—the very conditions McNally and Inayatullah argue may, ironically, result from developments in artificial intelligence and robotics.

Other cultures provide a view of civil rights that may better serve humans, nature, and robots alike. In cultures that do not elevate the status of the individual but value the collective, including nature, robots may be entitled to rights not because they are like humans but because they are part of the collective. In such cultures, relationships are exemplified by sharing, not dominating. Life exists for itself. Thus as robots become more intimately involved in the lives of humans and as people come to define differently what it means to be alive, attitudes toward robots will likely change. At present, however, even McNally and Inayatullah agree that extending rights to robots is, for most people, unthinkable. According to environmental lawyer Christopher S. Stone, "Throughout legal history, each successive extension of rights to some new entity has been, theretofore, a bit unthinkable. We are inclined to suppose the rightlessness of rightless 'things' to be a decree of Nature, not a legal convention acting in support of some status quo." Nevertheless, the futurists conclude, robotic technology is growing exponentially, making it difficult for institutions to keep pace. Thus, McNally and Inayatullah warn, "in order to minimize the stress caused by the expanding role of robotics, it is vital that the judiciary and legislators make proactive decisions and plan for the eventual development of robotic rights before the issue reaches a crisis point."

Whether legal systems will grant rights to robots remains to be seen. The authors in the following chapter present their views in related controversies surrounding the question: What ethical, legal, and moral issues relate to robotic technology? While the idea of robot rights may seem fantastic, McNally and Inayatullah conclude their analysis with the following caveat: "We must remember that the impossible is not always the fantastic and the fantastic not always the impossible."

"*Eventually the AI becomes sophisticated enough to start improving itself—not just small improvements but improvements large enough to cascade into other improvements . . . and the AI leaves our human abilities far behind.*"

Artificial Intelligence Will Exceed Human Intelligence

Luke Muehlhauser

Although few can imagine machines with greater-than-human intelligence, several characteristics of artificial intelligence (AI) suggest the very real possibility, argues Luke Muehlhauser in the following viewpoint. For example, he asserts, AI can send and receive signals faster and compute more rapidly than humans. Moreover, Muehlhauser maintains, machines, not limited by biology, can easily assess their own cognitive systems. Indeed, when machines discover how to improve themselves, their advanced replication ability will likely lead to an intelligence explosion— the singularity, in which AI exceeds human intelligence. Muehlhauser is executive director of the Machine Intelligence Research Institute, a Berkeley, California, think tank whose goal is to ensure that AI benefits humankind.

Luke Muehlhauser, "Plenty of Room Above Us" and "Intelligence Explosion," (two chapters) from *Facing the Intelligence Explosion*, 2013. Reproduced by permission.

As you read, consider the following questions:

1. In Muehlhauser's opinion, why is efficient cross-domain optimization not a natural plateau for intelligence?

2. According to the author, in what way is brain size and neuron count restrained in humans?

3. In the author's opinion, why does the *Homo* line of apes at first look much like any other brained animal?

W hy are AIs in movies so often of roughly human-level intelligence? One reason is that we almost *always* fail to see non-humans as non-human. We anthropomorphize. That's why aliens and robots in fiction are basically just humans with big eyes or green skin or some special power. Another reason is that it's hard for a writer to write characters that are smarter than the writer. How *exactly* would a superintelligent machine solve problem X? I'm not smart enough to know.

The human capacity for efficient cross-domain optimization[1] is not a natural plateau for intelligence. It's a narrow, accidental, temporary marker created by evolution due to things like the slow rate of neuronal firing and how large a skull can fit through a primate's birth canal. Einstein may *seem* "vastly" more intelligent than a village idiot, but this difference is dwarfed by the difference between the village idiot and a mouse.

As [computer scientist and sci-fi author] Vernor Vinge put it:

> The best answer to the question, "Will computers ever be as smart as humans?" is probably "Yes, but only briefly."

Surpassing Human Intelligence

How could an AI surpass human abilities? Let us count the ways. . . .

---

1. Cross-domain optimization is the ability to observe, learn, and act in different environments. At present, robots are generally programmed to operate in specific environments and cannot operate in different ones.

Speed. Our axons carry signals at 75 meters per second or slower. A machine can pass signals along about 4 million times more quickly.

Serial depth. The human brain can't rapidly perform any computation that requires more than 100 sequential steps; thus, it relies on massively parallel computation. More is possible when both parallel and deep serial computations can be performed.

Computational resources. The brain's size and neuron count are constrained by skull size, metabolism, and other factors. AIs could be built on the scale of buildings or cities or larger. When we can make circuits no smaller, we can just add more of them.

Rationality. . . . Human brains do nothing like optimal belief formation or goal achievement. Machines can be built from the ground up using (computable approximations of) optimal Bayesian decision networks,[2] and indeed this is already a leading paradigm in artificial agent design.

Introspective access / editability. We humans have almost no introspective access to our cognitive algorithms, and cannot easily edit and improve them. Machines can already do this (see EURISKO and metaheuristics). A limited hack like the method of loci[3] greatly improves human memory; machines can do this kind of thing in spades.

And this is only a partial list. Consider how far machines have surpassed our abilities at arithmetic, or how far they will surpass our abilities at chess or driving in another 20 years. There is no reason in principle why machines could not surpass our abilities at technology design or general reasoning by a similar margin. The human level is a minor pit-stop on the

---

2. A Bayesian decision network is a statistical model based on the probability of random variables and their conditional dependents. For example, if given a set of symptoms, a network can be used to compute the probabilities of various diseases.
3. Method of loci is a human memory enhancement tool, in which a person uses visualization to remember information.

The Importance of Addressing the Possibility of the Singularity

If there is a singularity, it will be one of the most important events in the history of the planet. An intelligence explosion has enormous potential benefits: a cure for all known diseases, an end to poverty, extraordinary scientific advances, and much more. It also has enormous potential dangers: an end to the human race, an arms race of warring machines, the power to destroy the planet. So if there is even a small chance that there will be a singularity, we would do well to think about what forms it might take and whether there is anything we can do to influence the outcomes in a positive direction.

David J. Chalmers,
"The Singularity: A Philosophical Analysis,"
Journal of Consciousness Studies, 2010.

way to the highest level of intelligence allowed by physics, and there is plenty of room above us. . . .

The Intelligence Explosion

Suppose you're a disembodied spirit watching the universe evolve. For the first 9 billion years, almost nothing happens.

"God, this is so *boring*!" you complain.

"How so?" asks your partner.

"There's no depth or complexity to anything because nothing *aims* at anything. Nothing *optimizes* for anything. There's no *plot*. It's just a bunch of random crap that happens. Worse than *Seinfeld*."[4]

4. *Seinfeld* was a popular situation comedy of the late 1980s and 1990s that was often referred to as "a show about nothing," as the show was driven more by character than plot.

"Really? What's that over there?"

You follow your partner's gaze and notice a tiny molecule in a pool of water on a rocky planet. Before your eyes, it makes a *copy* of itself. And then another. And then the copies make copies of themselves.

"A replicator!" you exclaim. "Within months there could be *millions* of those things."

"I wonder if this will lead to squirrels?"

"What are squirrels?"

Your partner explains the functional complexity of squirrels, which they encountered in Universe 217.

"That's *absurd*! At anything like our current rate of optimization, we wouldn't see any *squirrels* come about by pure accident until long after the heat death of the universe."

Superior Replications

But soon you notice something even more important: some of the copies are *errors*. The copies are exploring the neighboring regions of the conceptual search space. Some of these regions contain better replicators, and those superior replicators end up with more copies of themselves than the original replicators, and explore their own neighborhoods.

The next few billions years are by far the most exciting you've seen. Simple replicators lead to simple organisms, which lead to complex life, which leads to brains, which leads to the *Homo* line of apes.

At first, *Homo* looks much like any other brained animal. It shares 99% of its coding DNA with chimpanzees. You might be forgiven for thinking the human brain wasn't that big a deal—maybe it would enable a 50% increase in optimization speed, or something like that. After all, animal brains have been around for millions of years, and have gradually evolved without any dramatic increase in function.

But then, one thing leads to another. Before your eyes, humans become smart enough to domesticate crops, which leads to a sedentary lifestyle and repeatable trade, which leads to *writing* for keeping track of debts. Farming also generates food surpluses, and that enables professional specialization, which gives people the ability to focus on solving problems *other* than finding food. . . . Professional specialization leads to science and technology and the industrial revolution, which lead to space travel and iPhones.

Rewriting Algorithms

The difference between chimpanzees and humans illustrates how powerful it can be to rewrite an agent's cognitive algorithms. But of course, the algorithm's origin in this case was merely evolution, blind and stupid. An *intelligent* process with a bit of *foresight* can leap through the search space more efficiently. A human computer programmer can make innovations in a day that evolution couldn't have discovered in billions of years.

But for the most part, humans still haven't figured out how their *own* cognitive algorithms work, or how to rewrite them. And the computers we program don't understand *their* own cognitive algorithms, either (for the most part). But one day, they will.

Which means the future contains a feedback loop that the past does not:

> If you're EURISKO,[5] you manage to modify some of your metaheuristics, and the metaheuristics work noticeably better, and they even manage to make a few further modifications to themselves, but then the whole process runs out of steam and flatlines.

> It was human intelligence that produced these artifacts to begin with. Their *own* optimization power is far short of

5. EURISKO is a computer program that in lay terms can think outside of its domain by using heuristic—general rule or rule of thumb—thinking. The program was created by Douglas Lenat.

human—so incredibly weak that, after they push themselves along a little, they can't push any further. Worse, their optimization at any given level is characterized by a limited number of opportunities, which once used up are gone—extremely sharp diminishing returns. . . .

. . . When you first build an AI, it's a baby—if it had to improve itself, it would almost immediately flatline. So you push it along using your own cognition . . . and knowledge—*not* getting any benefit of recursion in doing so, just the usual human idiom of knowledge feeding upon itself and insights cascading into insights. Eventually the AI becomes sophisticated enough to start improving *itself*—not just small improvements, but improvements large enough to cascade into other improvements. . . . And then you get what I. J. Good called an "intelligence explosion."

. . . and the AI leaves our human abilities far behind.

At that point, we might as well be dumb chimpanzees watching as those new-fangled "humans" invent fire and farming and writing and science and guns and planes and take over the whole world. And like the chimpanzee, at that point we won't be in a position to negotiate with our superiors. Our future will depend on what *they* want.

> "By the end of the century, we believe, we will still be wondering if the singularity is near."

The Singularity Isn't Near

Paul G. Allen and Mark Greaves

Although machines may eventually exceed human intelligence, the breakthroughs necessary to understand the human brain will take much longer than futurists predict, claims Paul G. Allen and Mark Greaves in the following viewpoint. Making predictions based on exponential advancements in hardware is a flawed approach, they argue. Understanding human cognition is a much slower, more serendipitous process, the authors reason. Although efforts to understand how humans think continue, scientists will still be searching for answers at the end of the twenty-first century, they conclude. Allen, cofounder of Microsoft, is a philanthropist and chairman of Vulcan, a business investment company. Greaves is a computer scientist who serves as Vulcan's director for knowledge systems.

As you read, consider the following questions:

1. According to Allen and Greaves, how do the visions of futurists Vernor Vinge and Ray Kurzweil differ?

2. What do "brain duplication" strategies presuppose, in the authors' view?

3. In the authors' opinion, what is one answer to why it has proven so difficult for AI researchers to build human-like intelligence?

The Singularity Summit approaches this weekend in New York. But the Microsoft cofounder and a colleague say the singularity itself is a long way off.

Futurists like Vernor Vinge and Ray Kurzweil have argued that the world is rapidly approaching a tipping point, where the accelerating pace of smarter and smarter machines will soon outrun all human capabilities. They call this tipping point the *singularity*, because they believe it is impossible to predict how the human future might unfold after this point. Once these machines exist, Kurzweil and Vinge claim, they'll possess a superhuman intelligence that is so incomprehensible to us that we cannot even rationally guess how our life experiences would be altered. Vinge asks us to ponder the role of humans in a world where machines are as much smarter than us as we are smarter than our pet dogs and cats. Kurzweil, who is a bit more optimistic, envisions a future in which developments in medical nanotechnology will allow us to download a copy of our individual brains into these superhuman machines, leave our bodies behind, and, in a sense, live forever. It's heady stuff.

While we suppose this kind of singularity might one day occur, we don't think it is near. In fact, we think it will be a very long time coming. Kurzweil disagrees, based on his extrapolations about the rate of relevant scientific and technical progress. He reasons that the rate of progress toward the singularity isn't just a progression of steadily increasing capability, but is in fact exponentially accelerating—what Kurzweil calls the "Law of Accelerating Returns." He writes that:

So we won't experience 100 years of progress in the 21st century—it will be more like 20,000 years of progress (at today's rate). The "returns," such as chip speed and cost-effectiveness, also increase exponentially. There's even exponential growth in the rate of exponential growth. Within a few decades, machine intelligence will surpass human intelligence, leading to The Singularity . . .[1]

By working through a set of models and historical data, Kurzweil famously calculates that the singularity will arrive around 2045.

This prediction seems to us quite far-fetched. Of course, we are aware that the history of science and technology is littered with people who confidently assert that some event can't happen, only to be later proven wrong—often in spectacular fashion. We acknowledge that it is possible but highly unlikely that Kurzweil will eventually be vindicated. An adult brain is a finite thing, so its basic workings can ultimately be known through sustained human effort. But if the singularity is to arrive by 2045, it will take unforeseeable and fundamentally unpredictable breakthroughs, and not because the Law of Accelerating Returns made it the inevitable result of a specific exponential rate of progress.

Kurzweil's reasoning rests on the Law of Accelerating Returns and its siblings, but these are not physical laws. They are assertions about how past rates of scientific and technical progress can predict the future rate. Therefore, like other attempts to forecast the future from the past, these "laws" will work until they don't. More problematically for the singularity, these kinds of extrapolations derive much of their overall exponential shape from supposing that there will be a constant supply of increasingly more powerful computing capabilities. For the Law to apply and the singularity to occur circa 2045, the advances in capability have to occur not only in a computer's hardware technologies (memory, processing power, bus speed, etc.) but also in the software we create to run on these more capable computers. To achieve the singularity, it isn't enough to just run today's software faster. We would also need to build smarter and more capable software programs. Creating this kind of advanced software requires a prior scientific understanding of the foundations of human cognition, and we are just scraping the surface of this.

This prior need to understand the basic science of cognition is where the "singularity is near" arguments fail to persuade us. It is true that computer hardware technology can develop amazingly quickly once we have a solid scientific framework and adequate economic incentives. However, creating the software for a real singularity-level computer intelligence will require fundamental scientific progress beyond where we are today. This kind of progress is very different than the Moore's Law–style evolution of computer hardware capabilities that inspired Kurzweil and Vinge. Building the complex software that would allow the singularity to happen requires us to first have a detailed scientific understanding of how the human brain works that we can use as an architectural guide, or else create it all *de novo*. This means not just knowing the physical structure of the brain, but also how the brain reacts and changes, and how billions of parallel neuron interactions can result in human consciousness and original thought. Getting this kind of comprehensive understanding of the brain is not impossible. If the singularity is going to occur on anything like Kurzweil's timeline, though, then we absolutely require a massive acceleration of our scientific progress in understanding every facet of the human brain.

But history tells us that the process of original scientific discovery just doesn't behave this way, especially in complex areas like neuroscience, nuclear fusion, or cancer research. Overall scientific progress in understanding the brain rarely resembles an orderly, inexorable march to the truth, let alone an exponentially accelerating one. Instead, scientific advances are often irregular, with unpredictable flashes of insight punc-

The Challenging Road to the Singularity

The singularity is possible. It appears not to be imminent, which is probably good, since its arrival could be hugely detrimental to humanity, if the first AIs built are not ethical. However, we have technology in hand which promises good options tor implementing ethical AIs. We expect the road to the Singularity to be far more challenging than the Singularitarians expect. It will be more difficult than "mapping" the human brain: it will be at least as difficult as actually understanding it—that is, as understanding ourselves.

Kevin B. Korb and Ann E. Nicholson, The Cutting Edge, *March 6, 2012. www.thecuttingedgenews.com.*

tuating the slow grind-it-out lab work of creating and testing theories that can fit with experimental observations. Truly significant conceptual breakthroughs don't arrive when predicted, and every so often new scientific paradigms sweep through the field and cause scientists to reëvaluate portions of what they thought they had settled. We see this in neuroscience with the discovery of long-term potentiation, the columnar organization of cortical areas, and neuroplasticity. These kinds of fundamental shifts don't support the overall Moore's Law–style acceleration needed to get to the singularity on Kurzweil's schedule.

The Complexity Brake

The foregoing points at a basic issue with how quickly a scientifically adequate account of human intelligence can be developed. We call this issue the *complexity brake*. As we go deeper and deeper in our understanding of natural systems, we typically find that we require more and more specialized knowledge to characterize them, and we are forced to continuously expand our scientific theories in more and more complex ways. Understanding the detailed mechanisms of human cognition is a task that is subject to this complexity brake. Just think about what is required to thoroughly understand the human brain at a micro level. The complexity of the brain is simply awesome. Every structure has been precisely shaped by millions of years of evolution to do a particular thing, whatever it might be. It is not like a computer, with billions of identical transistors in regular memory arrays that are controlled by a CPU [central processing unit] with a few different elements. In the brain every individual structure and neural circuit has been individually refined by evolution and environmental factors. The closer we look at the brain, the greater the degree of neural variation we find. Understanding the neural structure of the human brain is getting harder as we learn more. Put another way, the more we learn, the more we realize there is to know, and the more we have to go back and revise our earlier understandings. We believe that one day this steady increase in complexity will end—the brain is, after all, a finite set of neurons and operates according to physical principles. But for the foreseeable future, it is the complexity brake and arrival of powerful new theories, rather than the Law of Accelerating Returns, that will govern the pace of scientific progress required to achieve the singularity.

So, while we think a fine-grained understanding of the neural structure of the brain is ultimately achievable, it has not shown itself to be the kind of area in which we can make exponentially accelerating progress. But suppose scientists make some brilliant new advance in brain scanning technology. Singularity proponents often claim that we can achieve computer intelligence just by numerically simulating the brain "bottom up" from a detailed neural-level picture. For example, Kurzweil predicts the development of nondestructive brain scanners that will allow us to precisely take a snapshot a person's living brain at the subneuron level. He suggests that these scanners would most likely operate from inside the brain via millions of injectable medical nanobots. But, regardless of whether nanobot-based scanning succeeds (and we aren't even close to knowing if this is possible), Kurzweil essentially argues that this is the needed scientific advance that will gate the singularity: computers could exhibit human-level intelligence simply by loading the state and connectivity of each of a brain's neurons inside a massive digital brain simulator, hooking up inputs and outputs, and pressing "start."

However, the difficulty of building human-level software goes deeper than computationally modeling the structural connections and biology of each of our neurons. "Brain duplication" strategies like these presuppose that there is no fundamental issue in getting to human cognition other than having sufficient computer power and neuron structure maps to do the simulation.[2] While this may be true theoretically, it has not worked out that way in practice, because it doesn't address everything that is actually needed to build the software. For example, if we wanted to build software to simulate a bird's ability to fly in various conditions, simply having a complete diagram of bird anatomy isn't sufficient. To fully simulate the flight of an actual bird, we also need to know how everything functions together. In neuroscience, there is a parallel situation. Hundreds of attempts have been made (using many different organisms) to chain together simulations of different neurons along with their chemical environment. The uniform result of these attempts is that in order to create an adequate simulation of the real ongoing neural activity of an organism, you also need a vast amount of knowledge about the *functional* role that these neurons play, how their connection patterns evolve, how they are structured into groups to turn raw stimuli into information, and how neural information processing ultimately affects an organism's behavior. Without this information, it has proven impossible to construct effective computer-based simulation models. Especially for the cognitive neuroscience of humans, we are not close to the requisite level of functional knowledge. Brain simulation projects underway today model only a small fraction of what neurons do and lack the detail to fully simulate what occurs in a brain. The pace of research in this area, while encouraging, hardly seems to be exponential. Again, as we learn more and more about the actual complexity of how the brain functions, the main thing we find is that the problem is actually getting harder.

The AI Approach

Singularity proponents occasionally appeal to developments in artificial intelligence (AI) as a way to get around the slow rate of overall scientific progress in bottom-up, neuroscience-based approaches to cognition. It is true that AI has had great successes in duplicating certain isolated cognitive tasks, most recently with IBM's Watson system for *Jeopardy!* question answering. But when we step back, we can see that overall AI-based capabilities haven't been exponentially increasing either, at least when measured against the creation of a fully general human intelligence. While we have learned a great deal about how to build individual AI systems that do seemingly intelligent things, our systems have always remained *brittle*—their performance boundaries are rigidly set by their internal assumptions and defining algorithms, they cannot generalize, and they frequently give nonsensical answers outside of their specific focus areas. A computer program that plays excellent chess can't leverage its skill to play other games. The best medical diagnosis programs contain immensely detailed knowledge of the human body but can't deduce that a tightrope walker would have a great sense of balance.

Why has it proven so difficult for AI researchers to build human-like intelligence, even at a small scale? One answer involves the basic scientific framework that AI researchers use. As humans grow from infants to adults, they begin by acquiring a general knowledge about the world, and then continuously augment and refine this general knowledge with specific knowledge about different areas and contexts. AI researchers have typically tried to do the opposite: they have built systems with deep knowledge of narrow areas, and tried to create a more general capability by combining these systems. This strategy has not generally been successful, although Watson's performance on *Jeopardy!* indicates paths like this may yet have promise. The few attempts that have been made to directly create a large amount of general knowledge of the world, and then add the specialized knowledge of a domain (for example, the work of Cycorp), have also met with only limited success. And in any case, AI researchers are only just beginning to theorize about how to effectively model the complex phenomena that give human cognition its unique flexibility: uncertainty, contextual sensitivity, rules of thumb, self-reflection, and the flashes of insight that are essential to higher-level thought. Just as in neuroscience, the AI-based route to achieving singularity-level computer intelligence seems to require many more discoveries, some new Nobel-quality theories, and probably even whole new research approaches that are incommensurate with what we believe now. This kind of basic scientific progress doesn't happen on a reliable exponential growth curve. So although developments in AI might ultimately end up being the route to the singularity, again the complexity brake slows our rate of progress, and pushes the singularity considerably into the future.

The amazing intricacy of human cognition should serve as a caution to those who claim the singularity is close. Without having a scientifically deep understanding of cognition, we can't create the software that could spark the singularity. Rather than the ever-accelerating advancement predicted by Kurzweil, we believe that progress toward this understanding is fundamentally slowed by the complexity brake. Our ability to achieve this understanding, via either the AI or the neuroscience approaches, is itself a human cognitive act, arising from the unpredictable nature of human ingenuity and discovery. Progress here is deeply affected by the ways in which our brains absorb and process new information, and by the creativity of researchers in dreaming up new theories. It is also governed by the ways that we socially organize research work in these fields, and disseminate the knowledge that results. At Vulcan and at the Allen Institute for Brain Science, we are working on advanced tools to help researchers deal with this daunting complexity, and speed them in their research. Gaining a comprehensive scientific understanding of human cognition is one of the hardest problems there is. We continue to make encouraging progress. But by the end of the century, we believe, we will still be wondering if the singularity is near.

Notes

1. Kurzweil, "The Law of Accelerating Returns," March 2001.

2. We are beginning to get within range of the computer power we might need to support this kind of massive brain simulation. Petaflop-class computers (such as IBM's BlueGene/P that was used in the Watson system) are now available commercially. Exaflop-class computers are currently on the drawing boards. These systems could probably deploy the raw computational capacity needed to simulate the firing patterns for all of a brain's neurons, though curently it happens many times more slowly than would happen in an actual brain.

> *"Much of the groundwork has already been laid for the sexual-robot craze to start."*

Sex with Robots Is Likely

David Levy

In the following viewpoint, David Levy maintains that although people today may find the idea absurd, in the future people will accept sex with robots. The fusion of sex and technology has indeed laid the groundwork for robot sex, he claims. While it might first only appeal to those on the fringes, as the media begins to normalize robot sex, the practice will expand, Levy asserts. In fact, robots might be the ideal solution when people have lost a long-term partner, as sexual intimacy takes years to evolve, and robots learn quickly to meet human needs, he suggests. Levy, an artificial intelligence expert, is author of Love and Sex with Robots.

As you read, consider the following questions:

1. What was the result of a February 2003 survey asking what sex technology most people desire, according to Levy?

David Levy, "Chapter 8: The Mental Leap to Sex with Robots," from *Love and Sex with Robots: The Evolution of Human-Robot Relationships*, New York: HarperCollins, 2007. Reproduced with permission.

2. What does Levy say that Maxwell Morris claims is the impact of expanding sexual freedom on what people view as normal in relationships?

3. In the author's opinion, what type of people will find it relatively easy to get used to the idea of robots as alternative sex partners?

In the early years of the twenty-first century, the idea of sex with robots is regarded by many people as outlandish, outrageous, even perverted. But sexual ideas, attitudes, and mores evolve with time, making it interesting to speculate on just how much current thinking needs to change before sex with robots is accepted as one of the normal expressions of human sexuality rather than one of its more bizarre offshoots and for us to ask what the processes will be that bring about such a change. . . .

The Cybersex Era

In two important respects, much of the groundwork has already been laid for the sexual-robot craze to start. First, sexual awareness and experiences are now happening to our children at ever-younger ages, a side effect of the revolution in sexual behavior in the second half of the twentieth century, of the ever-increasing media coverage of sex, and of the availability of pornography and other explicit sexual material on the Internet. The average age of first intercourse in the United Kingdom has fallen from twenty-one for women born in the 1930s to seventeen for those born in 1972. And Ward Elliott, quoting a long-unpublished 1970 Kinsey Institute survey, indicates that 92 percent of married American women who were born before 1900 were virgins at the time of their marriage, a figure that declined, on average, by about 8 percent per decade, to 30 percent for 1950s-born "disco era" women. This change is seen as even more dramatic when measured by the percentages of women who had had premarital sex, for whom the increase was almost ninefold, from 8 percent of women born in the nineteenth century to 70 percent of those born at the peak of the Baby Boom. Mirroring these changes, public tolerance of premarital intercourse has grown markedly since the 1960s. In 1969, 68 percent of the American public thought premarital coitus was wrong; this declined to 48 percent of the general population and only 19 percent of college students by 1975, a gap of only six years.

Just as the youth of today are becoming sexually active earlier than in any previous postwar [i.e., post–World War II] generation, the age at which children first learn about sex has lowered. Nowadays if a six-year-old tells his classmate that he has just found a condom on the patio, he is just as likely to be asked in reply, "What is a patio?" as "What is a condom?" Given this trend, it is reasonable to assume that society's attitudes on matters sexual will to a significant extent be more and more molded by the attitudes of the younger, sexually active generation.

The Marriage of Sex and Technology

Another development that lays the foundation for positive changes in attitude to sexual robots is the marriage of sex and technology, a union that started in the closing years of the twentieth century. One hundred years earlier, the invention of the automobile created a splendid venue for lovers lacking privacy, facilitating private assignation and fornication. And much more recently, sex has led some of the most important technological developments within the consumer-electronics industry, being, for instance, the driving force behind the boom in sales of the videocassette recorder (porn videos), then the DVD (more porn), and, of course, the Internet (yet more porn, and the first signs of interactive adult entertainment). These are examples of how social responses to technology sometimes encompass and encourage new sexual behaviors.

These two trends have fused together to create cybersex [sex involving computers or the Internet]. The usage of personal computers has become more and more the province of our youth, a phenomenon that will surely be repeated as hand-held PDAs [personal digital assistants] with wireless connections to the Internet and third-generation mobile phones both become mass-market consumer items for recreational use, including sex-related use. As our youth wholeheartedly embrace such technologies, so sex will increasingly permeate through to their computer screens and the liquid crystal displays (LCD) on their hand-held devices.

Android Love Slaves

When the Web site www.BetterHumans.com conducted a survey in February 2003 to investigate what sex technology most people desire, the clear favorite was "android love slaves" with 41 percent of the votes polled, followed at a discreet distance by mind-to-mind interfaces with 24 percent and virtual-reality sex with 17 percent. Clearly, robots are forming a significant part of the sexual thinking of the technologically aware. . . .

Before you get carried away with the idea that I intend to suggest that sex between two people will become outmoded, may I state very firmly that I do not believe for one moment that this will happen. What I *am* convinced of is that robot sex will become the only sexual outlet for *a few* sectors of the population—the misfits, the very shy, the sexually inadequate and uneducable—and that for some other sectors of the population robot sex will vary between something to be indulged in occasionally—when one's partner is away from home on a long trip, for example—to an activity that supplements one's regular sex life, perhaps when one's partner is not feeling well or not feeling like sex for some other reason.

Expanding Sexual Freedom

The modern era of expanding sexual freedom that began with the sexual revolution of the 1960s takes place in cultural environments typified by dynamic change and increased levels of social tolerance. Commenting in 1978 on some of the effects of this freedom on our view of what is normal in relationships, Maxwell Morris wrote:

> The dawning of a new idealism has given vent to increased sexual vigor and freedom among both sexes. The changing panoramic scenario of sexual liberation may, for example, be illustrated by the increasing number of non-traditional "experiments in living." Innovative living arrangements inclusive of the open marriage, group marriage, unmarried sexual cohabitation, and homosexual cohabitation offer a redefinition of the term "meaningful relationship."

Some of the effects of this same freedom on the sexual aspirations and fulfillment of the individual are described by Dennis Peck in terms of an increase in the potential of our sexual pleasure: "Individual fulfillment through various sexually related activities has resulted in a greater emphasis upon recreational sexual expressions." So in the case of technologically driven sexual practices, the ideas are already with us, even in advance of the general availability of the equipment that will turn these ideas into reality. . . .

When They Look Like Us

Some people will find it relatively easy to get used to the idea of robots as surrogate humans and alternative sex partners. In general I would expect these to be the technologically aware, those who grow up hand in hand with technology, those whose doubts and questions will relate more to what robots can and cannot do than to their appearance. This sector of society will find pleasure and excitement in exploring the capabilities of robots, including their emotional capacities, their personalities, and their sexual proficiencies and preferences.

Others—possibly because of deep reservations, possibly because of prejudice, possibly because their outlook is so literal that they will need to see realistic humanlike robots be-

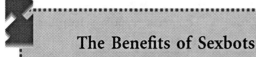

The Benefits of Sexbots

Sexbots will never have headaches, fatigue, impotence, premature ejaculation, pubic lice, disinterest, menstrual blood, jock strap itch, yeast infections, genital warts, AIDS/HIV, herpes, silly expectations, or inhibiting phobias. Sexbots will never stalk us, rape us, . . . weep when we dump them, or tell their friends we were boring in bed.

Hank Pellissier, Transhumanity, November 19, 2012.
http://transhumanity.net.

fore they can come to accept the concept of androids as pseudo peers—will take a lot more convincing. And to convince them, the appearance of the androids will be almost as important as, if not more important than, their technical capabilities. . . .

The Media Influence

As the first sexbots reach the market, the publicity for robot sex will take off with a bang. Initial news reports will most likely treat sexbots as a curiosity item, but this will not prevent their existence from becoming widely known. Very quickly, soft-core porn sites and Internet chat groups will start to display and discuss sexbots in action. As more and more people rush to their computer screens to watch others enjoying sex with robots, and as increasing numbers of sexual experimenters are interviewed by a medium anxious to publish all the voyeuristic and vicarious details of the thrills and joys of robot sex, so the mainstream media will stop blushing and cash in on the act. Just as *Marie Claire* published an article in 1994 on the almost unthinkable idea of women paying for sex and enjoying it, so the women's magazines of 2014, if not earlier, will, I am certain, be publishing articles on women's experiences in enjoying sex robots. The semiprivate, semipublic exhibition of teledildonics [electronic sex toys controlled by computer] that took place in 2005 at the New York Museum of Sex can be seen as a pioneering media event in this field. Only a few were able to be present in New York that night, or at the other end of the teledildonic line in San Francisco, but the event was reported in the online version of *Wired*, the highly respected, leading-edge high-tech magazine with a print circulation of more than half a million copies. When such events attract increasing amounts of attention from the mainstream media, albeit as curiosities at first, the idea of sexual robots will quickly spread. The first sexbots to reach the market will be too expensive for most to buy, or even to hire, so for a while these products will be restricted to the upper socioeconomic groups. But this was also true in the very early days of "home cinema" and in the early days of AIBO—Sony's robotic dog. As the media interest in robot sex grows, more people will try the experience, buying and hiring sexbots in numbers sufficient to bring down prices, thereby making sexbots available to men and women from a broader economic spectrum. . . .

The Benefits of Robot Sex

There are obvious social benefits in robot sex—the likely reduction in teenage pregnancy, abortions, sexually transmitted diseases, and pedophilia. And there are also clear personal benefits when sexual boundaries widen, ushering in new sexual opportunities, some bizarre, others exciting. In "Impacts of Robotic Sex," Joe Snell pointed to various ways in which robot sex could alter human relationships and human sexuality:

> Techno-virgins will emerge. An entire generation of humans may grow up never having had sex with other humans.

Heterosexual people may use same-sex sexbots to experiment with homosexual relations. Or gay people might use other-sex sexbots to experiment with heterosexuality.

Robotic sex may become "better" than human sex. Like many other technologies that have replaced human endeavors, robots may surpass human technique; because they would be programmable, sexbots would meet each individual's needs.

An important aspect of human sexuality is the possibility of failure or denial, making sex and the enjoyment of it somewhat capricious. In order to be better than human sex, the performance of sexbots might need to contain those subtleties of human sexuality that will enable them to mimic this capriciousness. Things that are always great can become boring, but the anticipation, doubt, and hope of each sexual experience can be instilled in their human owners if the sexbot is designed with these subtleties.

A Healthy Substitute

There are many professions that call for being absent from one's sex partner for varying periods of time. Robots can be the perfect substitutes in these situations, satisfying one's sexual needs without creating any cause for concern about disease and fidelity. For sailors, who a century ago would have been traditional customers for *dames de voyage* ["traveling ladies"—masturbatory sex dolls made of sewn cloth or old clothes, used by sailors during long voyages] a charming female robot would be a great alternative to masturbation or a visit to the local brothel when ashore. Ships' pursers will perhaps be loaning them out like library books, instead of administering penicillin jabs for the needy [to counteract sexually transmitted diseases].

There are many other situations in which a sexbot would be the ideal solution. For those who lose a spouse or a long-term partner, whether to illness, death, or as one of the casualties of a broken relationship, robots could provide the answer. As one ages, it becomes clear that maximal sexual intimacy sometimes takes a very long time to evolve—years, even—and that it redefines itself along the evolution of a loving relationship. Robots will be able to achieve this evolutionary process more quickly than humans, by retaining all the memories of living with their human other, analyzing the relationship characteristics exhibited by their human, and by themselves studying huge databases of relationships and how they are affected by different behaviors, then tuning their own behavior to the needs of their human mate. Humans often do not know what they really want or need, so intuitive robot sex partners are a real requirement, able to discern whether their owner really wants sex or would prefer a nice glass of wine or a walk in the park.

Thought-provoking? Certainly. But far-fetched? Not at all.

"With . . . android sex, there are no con-sequences, so bad behavior goes unpun-ished, reinforcing the behavior."

Sex with Robots Will Have Devastating Social Consequences

Rich Deem

In the following viewpoint, Rich Deem creates a hypothetical situation to illustrate the threat posed by robot sex. In his scenario, because more and more men choose sex with robots over relationships with women, marriage rates decline. As robot sex becomes accepted, manufacturers create robots that appeal to every sexual perversion, including sex with children and animals. Since robots comply with every wish, people also become more callous and rude. Since studies show that the widespread avail-ability of pornography has led to similar results, such predictions are not farfetched, he reasons. Deem is founder of Evidence for God from Science, a website that works to connect science and the Bible.

Rich Deem, "Why Sex with Robots Is Always Wrong: The Impending Demise of the Hu-man Species," godandscience.org, July 1, 2010. Reproduced by permission.

As you read, consider the following questions:

1. According to Deem's hypothetical, what breakthrough in computing leads to androids that are nearly indistinguishable from average human beings?

2. On what basis did prosecutors bring the author's hypothetical case of *City of Provo vs. FACA Entertainment* to court?

3. In the author's opinion, what did studies on the acceptance of pornography reveal about today's young adult males?

Brian was 28 when he bought his first FACA (female anatomically correct android). They had been around since the early 2020s, but had been much too expensive to personally own. Now that the price had dropped to around $80,000, Brian had thought that he would buy a car every 8–10 years, instead of every 4–5 years and new FACA in between. Besides, the new FACAs were much more realistic than the old ones, since the technology had developed to provide cooling to all the internal computers and simultaneously make the robot warm to the touch by providing fluidics through the computers to dissipate heat through a network of "capillaries" located just under the "skin." Yes, the new models were friendly *and* warm. Brian was introduced to FACAs in college, where the fraternities would rent a FACA during the weekends and go on binges of drinking and sex. The rental prices were rather high at first, since these FACAs were million-dollar machines, but eventually the supply caught up with demand and almost everybody could afford to rent or buy one.

Early FACA Design

Early attempts to create human-like robots were forced to rely upon microprocessor technology with large, heavy batteries that required frequent recharging. ASIMO, produced by

Honda, was the first robot to display human-like movement, but was capable of only an hour's operation before recharging its 17 pound battery pack. However, the invention of carbon nanotube-based computers increased the computing power, reduced power consumption, and decreased the weight of computing electronics. Coupled with rapid increases in speech recognition, the first human-like robots were soon being manufactured. Instead of magnesium frames covered with thick plastic, the robots were eventually designed using lightweight carbon-fiber composite designed to mimic the structure of human bones moved by pulley systems to generate the full range of human motion. The hard plastic was soon replaced with fabrics that felt like real skin. Thus, the transformation from machine to android was nearly complete.

From Good to Bad

Not content with merely an online presence, the adult entertainment industry soon realized that androids, properly constructed, could earn them billions of dollars in additional revenue. The first of these sex robots were crude, non-animated versions introduced in the early 2010s. However, soon top programmers and engineers were hired away from the automakers and computer companies with offers of up to ten times their average salaries, similar to what had been done with their movie businesses in the late 2010s, when they had hired away Hollywood's best CG [computer graphics] programmers to turn out realistic-looking virtual pornography movies. Of course, the acceptance of pornography as legitimate entertainment had rapidly escalated in the late 2000s, especially after Generation X had raised their own families. Although the newly designed FACA looked good, they were still somewhat clumsy and had trouble with all but the most common colloquialisms. For the average male college student, this was not a major problem, since conversation was not his major intent. However, when companies tried to market MACA, the male counterpart, to the female college crowd, the acceptance was less than stellar, although some women insisted that they weren't any worse at conversation than the average male. However, in the 2020s prices were way too high for all but the wealthy to purchase their own android.

Life in the 2030s

The breakthrough in computing came in the early 2030s when software engineers finally were able to design computers that could learn and interact in the way the human brain works. Coupled with individual nanotube computer-controlled joints, the androids were nearly indistinguishable from average human beings. Money from the adult entertainment industry, in their push for realistic motion and conversation, had accelerated the technology in what would have taken decades to only a few years. Mass production of FACAs rapidly brought down prices, and competition with mainstream entertainment providers, who didn't want to be left out of the rapidly expanding market, pushed prices further down. However, what had begun as merely weekend binges in college dorms and fraternities was brought to the mainstream. Acceptance among the male population evolved rapidly as men realized they could get an ideal "woman" whose only goal was to serve him. Entertainment companies became more bold as FACA were advertised as being "better than sex." In addition, FACA were adept at gourmet cooking, cleaning, and household chores, so that one could always use utility as an excuse to get one.

Opposition to FACA

As more and more men were able to purchase their own FACA, marriage rates dropped precipitously and women who were unable to find a real man turned to MACA or homosexuality in order to maintain relationships. The Church was inconsistently opposed to the whole FACA idea. After all, it wasn't like there was a specific commandment against having sex with a machine. An added bonus was that abortion virtually disappeared and out-of-wedlock pregnancies (in addition to any pregnancies at all) became very rare. Sperm banks sprang up all over as women who wanted to have children were forced to pay exorbitant prices, since very few men were interested in donating (even with the enticement of a free FACA rental for the purpose of donating at the sperm bank). Population control groups and environmentalists were thrilled that the human birth rate was now rapidly declining well below replacement levels. Several women's groups formed an alliance in an attempt to outlaw the sale of FACA. Virtually all attempts to legislate against FACA were either blocked by male legislators or in the courts as restricting freedom of speech. Finally, in the much watched case, *City of Provo vs. FACA Entertainment*, prosecutors attempted to get the practice outlawed on the basis of anti-slavery laws. In attempting to prove that FACA were intelligent beings that deserved protection from oppression under the Constitution of the United States, it seemed that the lawyers for the city were going to be able to prove their point, as they cross-examined a victim of FACA abuse. However, the defense brought in their own FACA to cross-examine. In the middle of the examination, the defense attorney suddenly grabbed the FACA and slammed it to the ground, scattering pieces of the machine all over the floor. Suddenly, the facade of humanity was gone, as the lawyer asked if anyone was going to charge him with a crime. The last challenge against the widespread use of FACA had been crushed.

Acceleration of Perversions

Initially, all FACA had been designed as young adult versions of their human counterparts. However, emboldened by their sweeping victories in the courts, FACA were soon designed as young girls and boys, and even animals, to meet every possible sexual perversion of their intended markets. Even those men who bought the adult FACA versions found their attitudes changing, since there were no consequences to anything they did with their FACA. After all, it didn't matter if you swore at your FACA or spoke harshly to it, since it always did exactly what you wanted. Over time, men who owned FACA became more and more rude to their human counterparts as the degradation of society accelerated. Men who owned a FACA disdained the company of real women, with all their incessant demands and mood swings. The sexual revolution was complete and we were all the victims.

Not Going to Happen?

Yes, the above scenario should bother you, whether you are a Christian or an atheist. Before you say that the scenario above is unlikely, I would like for you to consider some facts that led me to write the story and come to the belief that it is entirely possible that our societies could be headed in that direction. First, there are no legal barriers to the scenario playing out in full. The Supreme Court has ruled that nearly all forms of pornography are first amendment "protected speech." There is no reason to believe that a machine would not fall into that category. So there are no legal barriers. There are scientific barriers to robotic designs, but those are rapidly disappearing, as the first "FACA" are already being marketed.

Moral Acceptance

The data underlying the "radical" predictions laid out in this page come from scientific studies that have examined the pervasiveness and acceptance of pornography among today's young adults as "an acceptable way to express one's sexuality." For males the acceptance rate is 67% compared to 37% for their fathers. Among young adult women the acceptance rate is 49% compared to 20% among their mothers. So, the rate of acceptance of pornography has doubled in just one generation. When those young adults raise their own children, the acceptance rate will probably be greater than 80% for both males and females. The step between watching pornography through technology and engaging in sex acts through an attractive technological object is not that far, especially when the object *acts* as if it were a real human being.

Degradation of Attitudes and Morals

The idea that sex with robots will radically affect the attitudes of practitioners also comes from studies of those involved with pornography on a regular basis. Studies have found that viewing of pornography results in:

1. increased callousness toward women

2. trivialization of rape as a criminal offense

3. distorted perceptions about sexuality

4. increased appetite for more deviant and bizarre types of pornography (escalation and addiction)

5. devaluation of monogamy

6. decreased satisfaction with a partner's sexual performance, affection, and physical appearance

7. doubts about the value of marriage

8. decreased desire to have children

9. viewing non-monogamous relationships as normal and natural behavior

Pornography portrays an unrealistic view of relationships and persistent viewing enforces those views. An android that always does what it's told, despite bad behavior, enforces that behavior. In real relationships, bad behavior is thwarted through unpleasant consequences related to that behavior. With pornography and android sex, there are no consequences, so bad behavior goes unpunished, reinforcing the behavior.

What Can I Do?

The age of just accepting pornography as a harmless pastime has ended and people need to get serious about their personal and corporate responsibility toward opposing the spread of this evil and its soon-coming technological replacement. Revenue from pornography in 2006 was $97 billion worldwide. Every time you go online and view or download pornography somebody gets paid. It is time to stop that behavior and work toward the eradication of pornography. The Church must speak out forcefully against casual acceptance of pornography among its members. Get your pastor to speak about it. Have him read the above story in church. Yes, in church!

You atheists can't just sit around and snicker at it. Where are all the atheist organizations against the spread of pornography? You hold the truth in high esteem? Pornography is bad for people! As a seeker of truth and justice you should oppose things that are bad for people. Get it? Read the story to people among your groups. Report inappropriate content on mainstream websites. Get involved!

Conclusion

In case you didn't get it, this page is not about sex with robots at all. It is about increasing sexual perversion and increasingly pervasive virtual sex happening through the expanding acceptance of online pornography. Scientific studies show that those who consistently use pornography end up expressing increasingly antisocial behaviors. Since pornography is rapidly gaining acceptance among today's youth, it is likely that the world will become a more callous place as these attitudes become more acceptable. Sex with robots may or may not happen within the next 40 years, but we are definitely headed in that direction at present. The only thing holding it back at this point is the technology. Legal barriers do not exist, and moral barriers are eroding rapidly. Its advent will signal the impending end of the human race as 'perfect' mates replace the imperfect ones we now have. In order to stop this perversion from destroying the human race, we must act now to change attitudes toward virtual sex of all kinds, including pornography.

Note: I am in no way suggesting that robotic technology is evil in itself. I only object to the use of robotic technology for evil purposes, which would include its use as a surrogate for human relationships or to subjugate or murder humans. In other words, not every use of robotic technology is morally acceptable.

References

1. Firm unveils X-rated robot (PhysOrg.com)

2. A study published in 2008 showed that 49% of women and 67% of men aged 18-26 considered pornography "an acceptable way to express one's sexuality" compared to only 37% of their fathers and 20% of their mothers. Carroll, J. S., Padilla-Walker, L. M., Nelson, L. J., Olson, C. D., McNamara Barry, C., and Madsen, S. D. 2008. Generation XXX: Pornography Acceptance and Use Among Emerging Adults. *Journal of Adolescent Research* 23: 6–30.

3. Drake, R. E. 1994. Potential health hazards of pornography consumption as viewed by psychiatric nurses. *Archives of Psychiatric Nursing* 8: 101–106; Zillman, D., & Bryant, J. 1982. Pornography, sexual callousness, and the trivialization of rape. *Journal of Communication* 32: 10–21; Zillman, D., & Bryant, J. 1984. Effects of massive exposure to pornography. In N.M. Malamuth & E. Donnerstein (Eds.), *Pornography and Sexual Aggressionimg*, Orlando, FL: Academic, pp. 115–138; Zillman, D., & Bryant, J. 1988. Effects of prolonged consumption of pornography on family values. *Journal of Family Issues* 9: 518–544.

| "As machines with limited autonomy operate . . . in open environments, it becomes increasingly important to design a kind of functional morality that is sensitive to ethically relevant features of [given] situations."

Engineering Morality into Robots Will Be Necessary

Colin Allen

Rapid advances in cognitive science and the development of autonomous machines suggest active exploration of machine morality, argues Colin Allen in the following viewpoint. Although some assert that robots only do what they are told, when machine intelligence approaches human intelligence and human interaction with machines increases, machines must make ethical decisions, he claims. Human intelligence is more than a computational process: resolving ambiguous ethical situations requires a philosophical not a computational process, Allen asserts. Moreover, he concludes, designing moral machines will increase human understanding. Allen, director of the Cognitive Science program at Indiana University, coauthored Moral Machines *with Wendell Wallach.*

Professor Colin Allen, "The Future of Moral Machines," *New York Times*, December 25, 2011. Reproduced with permission.

As you read, consider the following questions:

1. In Allen's view, what do Singularitarians assume about artificial intelligence?

2. What examples does the author give that machines are increasingly operating with minimal human oversight?

3. In the author's opinion, what might building artificial moral agents forestall?

A robot walks into a bar and says, "I'll have a screwdriver." A bad joke, indeed. But even less funny if the robot says "Give me what's in your cash register."

The fictional theme of robots turning against humans is older than the word itself, which first appeared in the title of Karel Čapek's 1920 play about artificial factory workers rising against their human overlords. Just 22 years later, [science fiction writer] Isaac Asimov invented the "Three Laws of Robotics" to serve as a hierarchical ethical code for the robots in his stories: first, never harm a human being through action or inaction; second, obey human orders; last, protect oneself. From the first story in which the laws appeared, Asimov explored their inherent contradictions. Great fiction, but unworkable theory.

The Development of Intelligent Machines

The prospect of machines capable of following moral principles, let alone understanding them, seems as remote today as the word "robot" is old. Some technologists enthusiastically extrapolate from the observation that computing power doubles every 18 months to predict an imminent "technological singularity" in which a threshold for machines of superhuman intelligence will be suddenly surpassed. Many Singularitarians assume a lot, not the least of which is that intelligence is fundamentally a computational process. The techno-optimists among them also believe that such machines will be essentially friendly to human beings. I am skeptical about the Singularity, and even if "artificial intelligence" is not an oxymoron, "friendly A.I." will require considerable scientific progress on a number of fronts.

The neuro- and cognitive sciences are presently in a state of rapid development in which alternatives to the metaphor of mind as computer have gained ground. Dynamical systems theory, network science, statistical learning theory, developmental psychobiology and molecular neuroscience all challenge some foundational assumptions of A.I., and the last 50 years of cognitive science more generally. These new approaches analyze and exploit the complex causal structure of physically embodied and environmentally embedded systems, at every level, from molecular to social. They demonstrate the inadequacy of highly abstract algorithms operating on discrete symbols with fixed meanings to capture the adaptive flexibility of intelligent behavior. But despite undermining the idea that the mind is fundamentally a digital computer, these approaches have improved our ability to use computers for more and more robust simulations of intelligent agents—simulations that will increasingly control machines occupying our cognitive niche. If you don't believe me, ask Siri.[1]

This is why, in my view, we need to think long and hard about machine morality. Many of my colleagues take the very idea of moral machines to be a kind of joke. Machines, they insist, do only what they are told to do. A bar-robbing robot would have to be instructed or constructed to do exactly that. On this view, morality is an issue only for creatures like us who can choose to do wrong. People are morally good only insofar as they must overcome the urge to do what is bad. We can be moral, they say, because we are free to choose our own paths.

---

1. Siri is a voice recognition software program for Apple i-operating systems that understands natural speech and asks additional information if it needs more information to complete tasks.

There are big themes here: freedom of will, human spontaneity and creativity, and the role of reason in making good choices—not to mention the nature of morality itself. Fully human-level moral agency, and all the responsibilities that come with it, requires developments in artificial intelligence or artificial life that remain, for now, in the domain of science fiction. And yet . . .

The Growth of Autonomous Machines

Machines are increasingly operating with minimal human oversight in the same physical spaces as we do. Entrepreneurs are actively developing robots for home care of the elderly. Robotic vacuum cleaners and lawn mowers are already mass-market items. Self-driving cars are not far behind. Mercedes is equipping its 2013 model S-Class cars with a system that can drive autonomously through city traffic at speeds up to 25 m.p.h. Google's fleet of autonomous cars has logged about 200,000 miles without incident in California and Nevada, in conditions ranging from surface streets to freeways. By Google's estimate, the cars have required intervention by a human co-pilot only about once every 1,000 miles and the goal is to reduce this rate to once in 1,000,000 miles. How long until the next bank robber will have an autonomous getaway vehicle?

This is autonomy in the engineer's sense, not the philosopher's. The cars won't have a sense of free will, not even an illusory one. They may select their own routes through the city but, for the foreseeable future, they won't choose their own paths in the grand journey from dealership to junkyard. We don't want our cars leaving us to join the Peace Corps, nor will they any time soon. But as the layers of software pile up between us and our machines, they are becoming increasingly independent of our direct control. In military circles, the phrase "man on the loop" has come to replace "man in the loop," indicating the diminishing role of human overseers in

Developing Ethics for Advanced Artificial Intelligence

Humans, the first general intelligences to exist on Earth, have used that intelligence to substantially reshape the globe—carving mountains, taming rivers, building skyscrapers, farming deserts, producing unintended planetary climate changes. A more powerful intelligence could have correspondingly larger consequences. . . .

Considering the ethical history of human civilizations over centuries of time, we can see that it might prove a very great tragedy to create a mind that was *stable* in ethical dimensions along which human civilizations seem to exhibit *directional change*. . . .

This presents us with perhaps the ultimate challenge of machine ethics. How do you build an AI [artificial intelligence] which, when it executes, becomes more ethical than you? . . .

If we are serious about developing advanced AI, this is a challenge that we must meet. If machines are to be placed in a position of being stronger, faster, more trusted, or smarter than humans, then the discipline of machine ethics must commit itself to seeking human-superior (not just human-equivalent) niceness.

Nick Bostrom and Eliezer Yudkowsky,
Cambridge Handbook of Artificial Intelligence, *2011.*

controlling drones and ground-based robots that operate hundreds or thousands of miles from base. These machines need to adjust to local conditions faster than can be signaled and processed by human tele-operators. And while no one is yet recommending that decisions to use lethal force should be handed over to software, the Department of Defense is sufficiently committed to the use of autonomous systems that it has sponsored engineers and philosophers to outline prospects for ethical governance of battlefield machines.

Designing Moral Machines

Joke or not, the topic of machine morality is here to stay. Even modest amounts of engineered autonomy make it necessary to outline some modest goals for the design of artificial moral agents. Modest because we are not talking about guidance systems for the Terminator or other technology that does not yet exist. Necessary, because as machines with limited autonomy operate more often than before in open environments, it becomes increasingly important to design a kind of functional morality that is sensitive to ethically relevant features of those situations. Modest, again, because this functional morality is not about self-reflective moral agency— what one might call "full" moral agency—but simply about trying to make autonomous agents better at adjusting their actions to human norms. This can be done with technology that is already available or can be anticipated within the next 5 to 10 years.

The project of designing artificial moral agents provokes a wide variety of negative reactions, including that it is preposterous, horrendous, or trivial. My co-author Wendell Wallach and I have been accused of being, in our book *Moral Machines*, unimaginatively human-centered in our views about morality, of being excessively optimistic about technological solutions, and of putting too much emphasis on engineering the machines themselves rather than looking at the whole context in which machines operate.

In response to the charge of preposterousness, I am willing to double down. Far from being an exercise in science fiction, serious engagement with the project of designing artificial moral agents has the potential to revolutionize moral philosophy in the same way that philosophers' engagement with science continuously revolutionizes human self-understanding. New insights can be gained from confronting the question of whether and how a control architecture for robots might utilize (or ignore) general principles recommended by major ethical theories. Perhaps ethical theory is to moral agents as physics is to outfielders—theoretical knowledge that isn't necessary to play a good game. Such theoretical knowledge may still be useful after the fact to analyze and adjust future performance.

Building Ethically Sensitive Machines

Even if success in building artificial moral agents will be hard to gauge, the effort may help to forestall inflexible, ethically-blind technologies from propagating. More concretely, if cars are smart enough to navigate through city traffic, they are certainly smart enough to detect how long they have been parked outside a bar (easily accessible through the marriage of G.P.S. and the Internet) and to ask you, the driver, to prove you're not drunk before starting the engine so you can get home. For the near term (say, 5 to 10 years), a responsible human will still be needed to supervise these "intelligent" cars, so you had better be sober. Does this really require artificial morality, when one could simply put a breathalyzer between key and ignition? Such a dumb, inflexible system would have a kind of operational morality in which the engineer has decided that no car should be started by person with a certain blood alcohol level. But it would be ethically blind—incapable, for instance, of recognizing the difference between, on the one hand, a driver who needs the car simply to get home and, on the other hand, a driver who had a couple of drinks with dinner but needs the car because a 4-year old requiring urgent medical attention is in the back seat.

It is within our current capacities to build machines that are able to determine, based on real-time information about current traffic conditions and access to actuarial tables, how likely it is that this situation might lead to an accident. Of course, this only defers the ethical question of how to weigh the potential for harm that either option presents, but a well-designed system of human-machine interaction could allow for a manual override to be temporarily logged in a "black-box" similar to those used on airplanes. In case of an accident this would provide evidence that the person had taken responsibility. Just as we can envisage machines with increasing degrees of autonomy from human oversight, we can envisage machines whose controls involve increasing degrees of sensitivity to things that matter ethically. Not perfect machines, to be sure, but better.

A Philosophical Middle Space

Does this talk of artificial moral agents overreach, contributing to our own dehumanization, to the reduction of human autonomy, and to lowered barriers to warfare? If so, does it grease the slope to a horrendous, dystopian future? I am sensitive to the worries, but optimistic enough to think that this kind of technopessimism has, over the centuries, been oversold. Luddites [people opposed to technological change] have always come to seem quaint, except when they were dangerous. The challenge for philosophers and engineers alike is to figure out what should and can reasonably be done in the middle space that contains somewhat autonomous, partly ethically-sensitive machines. Some may think the exploration of this space is too dangerous to allow. Prohibitionists may succeed in some areas—robot arms control, anyone?—but they will not, I believe, be able to contain the spread of increasingly autonomous robots into homes, eldercare, and public spaces, not to mention the virtual spaces in which much software already operates without a human in the loop. We want machines that do chores and errands without our having to monitor them continuously. Retailers and banks depend on software controlling all manner of operations, from credit card purchases to inventory control, freeing humans to do other things that we don't yet know how to construct machines to do.

Where's the challenge, a software engineer might ask? Isn't ethical governance for machines just problem-solving within constraints? If there's fuzziness about the nature of those constraints, isn't that a philosophical problem, not an engineering one? Besides, why look to human ethics to provide a gold standard for machines? My response is that if engineers leave it to philosophers to come up with theories that they can implement, they will have a long wait, but if philosophers leave it to engineers to implement something workable they will likely be disappointed by the outcome. The challenge is to reconcile these two rather different ways of approaching the world, to yield better understanding of how interactions among people and contexts enable us, sometimes, to steer a reasonable course through the competing demands of our moral niche. The different kinds of rigor provided by philosophers and engineers are both needed to inform the construction of machines that, when embedded in well-designed systems of human-machine interaction, produce morally reasonable decisions even in situations where Asimov's laws would produce deadlock.

> *"Drone technology dramatically enhances the government's ability to monitor citizens in public places and on their own property—and privacy law hasn't kept pace with technological change."*

Police Use of Unmanned Aircraft Raises Privacy Concerns

Gene Healy

Although Americans do not have any expectation of privacy in public spaces, the domestic use of unmanned aircraft to monitor citizens raises some serious questions, argues Gene Healy in the following viewpoint. These aircraft, also known as drones, use technology that significantly enhances police power to monitor Americans in public and at home, he maintains. Unfortunately, Healy argues, privacy law has not kept pace with drone technology. Public opposition to drone surveillance may be necessary to improve US privacy laws, he reasons. Healy is a vice president at the Cato Institute, a libertarian think tank, whose research interests include executive power, federalism, and overcriminalization.

As you read, consider the following questions:

1. In Healy's opinion, at the time of this writing, how many drones does law enforcement already have?

2. What was the result of a Rasmussen poll in February 2012, according to the author?

3. What did James Madison warn at the Constitutional Convention, according to Healy?

Last week [in June 2012], in its report on the 2013 Defense Authorization bill, the Senate Armed Services Committee called for allowing drones [UAVs] to operate "freely and routinely" in U.S. airspace.

"Large numbers of [UAVs] now deployed overseas may be returned to the United States as the conflict in Afghanistan and operations elsewhere wind down in coming years," the Committee Report read.

Drones "have clearly demonstrated their immense value to DOD [Department of Defense] military capabilities in the global war on terrorism," and they're increasingly "contributing to missions of agencies and departments within the United States.... The pace of development must be accelerated," the report concluded.

War Technology Is Coming Home

Technology forged for gathering battlefield intelligence and waging war against terrorists is coming home—and the powers that be seem pretty blithe about it.

"It's great!" Virginia Gov. Bob McDonnell said on WTOP's "Ask the Governor" program last month: "That's why we use [UAVs] on the battlefield.... If you're keeping police officers safe, making it more productive and saving money ... it's absolutely the right thing to do."

"Drones," cartoon by David Fitzsimmons, *Arizona Star*, June 5, 2012. Copyright © 2012 by David Fitzsimmons and Cagle Cartoons.

"Drones are a legitimate form of law enforcement," Rep. Peter King, R-N.Y., told CNN's Candy Crowley: "You don't have an expectation of privacy if you're in the open."

True enough: as Stanford Law's Ryan Calo notes, under current law, "citizens do not enjoy a reasonable expectation of privacy in public, nor even on the portions of their property visible from a public vantage."

Monitoring Citizens

That's a problem. Drone technology dramatically enhances the government's ability to monitor citizens in public places and on their own property—and privacy law hasn't kept pace with technological change.

Law enforcement agencies already have access to some 146 commercial drones—and that may be just the beginning as drones get smaller and more capable.

Defense contractor AeroVironment is perfecting the "Nano Hummingbird," a drone that weighs less than an AA battery and is capable of alighting on a window ledge to record video.

The "Gorgon Stare" system, under development by the Air Force, features a drone-mounted, Argus-eyed camera array designed for full-spectrum surveillance.

"Gorgon Stare will be looking at a whole city, so there will be no way for the adversary to know what we're looking at, and we can see everything," an Air Force officer bragged to the *Washington Post*. "The Department of Homeland Security is exploring the technology's potential, an industry official said."

Updating Privacy Laws

Creepy? Sure. But the dystopian fears these metal sentinels provoke might force us to get serious about new legal protections. Privacy violations in the form of massive data mining and the like "tend to be hard to visualize," Stanford's Professor Calo observes. The specter of domestic drones "could be just the visceral jolt society needs to drag privacy law into the 21st century."

Indeed, Americans are becoming increasingly unsettled by this sort of military "mission creep." In February [2012], a Rasmussen poll found voters opposed to the use of drones for domestic surveillance, 52 to 30.

Some legislators are taking note. Last week, Rep. Austin Scott, R-G.A., introduced a bill to restrict domestic use of drones. His "Preserving Freedom From Unwarranted Surveillance Act" leaves space for legitimate public safety uses of UAVs in "exigent circumstances" like hostage situations or missing person hunts. But it provides that "a person or entity acting under the authority of the United States shall not use a drone to gather evidence or other information except to the extent authorized in a warrant."

That's a start—but we'll need continual vigilance to ensure that technologies developed for foreign wars aren't turned into tools of domestic social control. As James Madison warned at the Constitutional Convention, "The means of defense against foreign danger have always been the instruments of tyranny at home."

> *"The drone is potentially a powerful tool. Vigilance is advisable; panic is silly."*

The Great Drone Panic

Rich Lowry

Opponents overstate fears concerning the domestic use of unmanned aircraft, argues Rich Lowry in the following viewpoint. Many object to these aircraft, also known as drones, because they are also used as weapons of war, he maintains. However, Lowry claims, police use other weapons of war such as firearms and helicopters without such objections. Police must of course ensure that the domestic law enforcement use of drones respects constitutional rights, he concedes. However, he reasons, in the end, how police use the technology, not the technology itself, calls for caution. Lowry is editor of National Review, *a conservative American newsmagazine.*

As you read, consider the following questions:

1. What does Senator Rand Paul consider the danger posed by drones, according to Lowry?

2. In the author's opinion, as what is the fear of drones masquerading?

3. According to the *New York Times* as cited by Lowry, how is the market for drones expected to change?

The Great Drone Panic of 2012 is upon us.

Congress recently instructed the Federal Aviation Administration to open up the skies to more domestic use of the pilotless aircraft by private citizens and law enforcement. This, we're told in the urgent tones of Paul Revere on his famous ride, is the first step toward a dystopian surveillance state overseen by a ubiquitous drone air force. Nothing will be hidden from the watchful eye of the drones.

The influential conservative columnist Charles Krauthammer wants drones banned domestically and thinks the first American to shoot one down will be declared a national hero. Senator Rand Paul considers them a clear-and-present danger to American freedom and is offering legislation to require a warrant every time one takes flight, except to patrol the border or in extraordinary circumstances. The drone is to our liberty what the wolf is to sheep, a natural enemy.

It is understandable that drones don't have a warm-and-fuzzy image. Overseas, they are vehicles for an ongoing campaign of assassination. The drone attack has become the signature tactic in the war against terror. Spectacularly precise strikes take out people who had no idea they were coming, in notably antiseptic (for the operator of the drone, at least) acts of warfare.

And this is the first objection to the use of drones domestically: They are weapons of war! About to be deployed here at home! Not exactly. We don't kill people with drones; we kill them with Hellfire missiles. The drone is just the platform. By this standard, we would have no police helicopters because helicopters are weapons of war. For that matter, by this standard police shouldn't be allowed to carry firearms, which are a weapon of war going back a couple of centuries.

As for police drones randomly watching us as we innocently go about our business, this is not a novel phenomenon. Police do it all the time. It is called a patrol. They do it utilizing all manner of technology—on foot, on horseback, on bikes, in cars, and even on Segway scooters. So long as they are looking at us in public areas where we have no reasonable expectation of privacy, our liberty survives intact.

Drones will no doubt raise novel issues under the Fourth Amendment, which prohibits unreasonable search and seizure. They will require rules. The same is true of any technology, of course. The Supreme Court held unanimously earlier this year that police can't attach a GPS tracker on someone's vehicle without a warrant. This isn't reason to ban all use of GPS trackers by law enforcement. The fear of drones is, in part, the fear of the new—it is Luddism masquerading as civil libertarianism.

Drones are coming no matter what. They will be too inexpensive and too useful to ignore. FedEx and UPS are interested in using drones to fly cargo. Farmers have used drones to monitor their crops. The market for drones, now almost $6 billion, is expected to double in the next ten years, according to the *New York Times*. Lockheed Martin is developing a tiny drone inspired by the aerodynamics of a maple seed that could fly around inside buildings.

As drones proliferate for commercial and other private uses, it is foolish to expect law enforcement to forgo them. Already, the Border Patrol uses drones down at the border. One day we will marvel that there was a time when a police drone wasn't first on the scene of a shooting. Or a time when we had high-speed car chases, endangering everyone else on the road, instead of a drone following the suspect from the air.

Ultimately, it is not the technology that matters, but the use to which it is put. A can of pepper spray is technologically unsophisticated. Yet it can be an instrument of cruelty if wielded arbitrarily by a cop. The drone is potentially a powerful tool. Vigilance is advisable; panic is silly.

Periodical and Internet Sources Bibliography

The following articles have been selected to supplement the diverse views presented in this chapter.

Thomas R. Eddlem	"Drones over America," *New American*, May 9, 2012.
Adam Gopnik	"Get Smart: How Will We Know When Machines Are More Intelligent than We Are?," *New Yorker*, April 4, 2011.
Kevin B. Korb and Ann E. Nicholson	"Ethics of a Technological Singularity: Will Robots Rule?," Spero News, March 8, 2012. www.speroforum.com.
Ray Kurzweil	"Kurzweil Responds: Don't Underestimate the Singularity," *Technology Review*, October 20, 2011.
Charles T. Rubin	"Machine Morality and Human Responsibility," *New Atlantis*, Summer 2011.
Subhranshu Sekhar Samal, Atirek Wribhu, and S. Sathyamurthy	"Artificial Intelligence Meets the Real World," *Electronics for You*, October 2, 2011.
Space Daily	"Caltech Researchers Create the First Artificial Neural Network out of DNA," August 3, 2011. www.spacedaily.com.
Andrea Stone	"Drone Program Aims to 'Accelerate' Use of Unmanned Aircraft by Police," *Huffington Post*, May 22, 2012. www.huffingtonpost.com.
Bob Unruh	"Civil Rights Advocates Trying to 'Shoot Down' Drones," WND, June 2012. www.wnd.com.

For Further Discussion

Chapter 1

1. Wendell Wallach and Colin Allen claim that robots may pose a threat to humankind, as programming robots to operate ethically in an unpredictable future may not be possible. What is the authors' view of humanity and how does this view inform their rhetoric? Explain your answer.

2. Some fear that robots will take human jobs. Erik Brynjolfsson and Andrew McAfee claim, however, that while robots can do many things, they cannot come up with original, inventive ideas or products. Farhad Manjoo counters that robots nonetheless increasingly perform higher-skilled jobs, posing a threat to those who have made a significant investment in education. Identify the types of evidence the authors use to support their arguments. Which type of evidence do you find most persuasive? Explain.

3. Ben Hargreaves asserts that robot doctors cannot replace human doctors but claims that robots can allow doctors to consult in remote locations and improve their surgical performance. Rebecca Hendren does not dispute that robots may be useful in the operating theater but argues instead that the role of nurses in general is misunderstood and that nurses have skills that robots do not. Both viewpoints were written for trade publications. How does the audience for each viewpoint influence each author's rhetoric?

4. Ian A. Crawford maintains that human explorers will perform better in space than robots will. Chad Orzel claims, on the other hand, that robot space explorers can, like humans, make serendipitous discoveries and solve problems at a significantly lower cost. What evidence does each

author provide to support his claim? Does this evidence make one viewpoint more persuasive than the other, in your opinion? Explain.

5. Of the robotic technology benefits explored in this chapter, which do you think will be most beneficial? Which do you think poses the greatest risk, if any? Explain.

Chapter 2

1. Joseph W. Dyer argues that robots will play a critical role in future armed conflicts. Dyer's view reflects the tactical needs of warfare. How does this aspect of war influence the evidence the author uses to support his view? Do you agree with his view? Why or why not?

2. Charles G. Kels claims that drone technology is an effective tool in the fight against terrorism and that the use of drones is legal. Paul Sullivan asserts that drones are only a partial solution. To truly fight terrorism, Sullivan argues, the United States must address the socioeconomic conditions that allow terrorists to function. Note the authors' affiliations. How do their affiliations influence their rhetoric? Which rhetorical strategy do you find more persuasive? Why?

3. Noel Sharkey has little confidence that autonomous robot warriors will be able to make the complex ethical decisions necessary to take a human life. Thus, he maintains, new international laws of war to guide the use of robot warriors will be necessary. Ronald C. Arkin agrees that ethics must guide the development of robot warriors, but he claims that robots may be better able to make complex ethical decisions under stress than human soldiers can. Both authors are robotic engineers yet appear to have different opinions about the decision-making skills of humans and robots. How are these opinions reflected in the evidence they provide? Which do you find more persuasive? Explain.

4. Stew Magnuson suggests that the military establishment is slow to accept robots as partners in armed conflict. Magnuson suggests strategies to help overcome this reluctance. Which viewpoints in this chapter do you think will influence military decision-makers to accept robotic technology? What arguments and evidence led you to this conclusion?

Chapter 3

1. Luke Muehlhauser maintains that artificial intelligence (AI) has characteristics that make it likely that AI will exceed human intelligence. Paul G. Allen and Mark Greaves do not dispute that AI may ultimately exceed human intelligence; they claim, however, that the complexity of human thought make such an event a long way off. Note the authors' affiliations. How do their affiliations influence their rhetoric? Which rhetorical strategy do you find more persuasive? Explain.

2. David Levy argues that robot sex will eventually become an accepted practice for the same sociocultural reasons that other sexual practices once considered inappropriate became acceptable. Rich Deem does not dispute this possibility. Instead, he argues that robot sex poses a serious threat to humanity. Identify each author's background, rhetorical style, and strategy. How does this strategy influence the evidence each author uses to support his view? Which do you find more persuasive and why?

3. Colin Allen asserts that as robot intelligence and interaction with humans grows, so will the need to create moral robots. Robotics is often described as the fusion of mechanical engineering and the study of artificial intelligence. What scientific discipline does the author represent? Might this influence the author's view? Explain.

4. Gene Healy believes that the domestic use of unmanned aircraft requires that policy makers revisit privacy laws.

Rich Lowry believes that opponents of law enforcement's use of unmanned aircraft are overreacting. What evidence does each author provide to support his claim? Which do you find more persuasive? Explain.

5. What commonalities among the evidence and rhetoric can you find in the viewpoints on both sides of the debate in this chapter? What impact do these strategies have on the viewpoints' persuasiveness? Explain.

Organizations to Contact

The editors have compiled the following list of organizations concerned with the issues debated in this book. The descriptions are derived from materials provided by the organizations. All have publications or information available for interested readers. The list was compiled on the date of publication of the present volume; the information provided here may change. Be aware that many organizations take several weeks or longer to respond to inquiries, so allow as much time as possible.

The Association for the Advancement of Artificial Intelligence (AAAI)

2275 E. Bayshore Rd., Ste. 160, Palo Alto, CA   94303
(650) 328-3123 • fax: (650) 321-4457
website: www.aaai.org

AAAI advances the understanding of the mechanisms underlying thought and intelligent behavior and their embodiment in machines. The association publishes the quarterly *AI Magazine* for members but also provides access to resources concerning artificial intelligence for those who would like to learn about AI under its AITopics link on its website, including "The Future of Moral Machines" and "More Jobs Predicted for Machines, Not People." Website visitors can read news stories about AI in "AI in the News" or in any of the RSS feeds associated with individual topics.

Association for Unmanned Vehicle Systems International (AUVSI)

2700 S. Quincy St., Ste. 400, Arlington, VA   22206
(703) 845-9671 • fax: (703) 845-9679
e-mail: info@auvsi.org
website: www.auvsi.org

AUVSI is a membership organization that promotes unmanned systems and related technology. Members represent government organizations, industry, and academia and support the defense, civil, and commercial sectors. AUVSI publishes the monthly *Unmanned Systems*, which highlights current global developments and unveils new technologies in air, ground, maritime, and space systems.

Brookings Institution

1775 Massachusetts Ave. NW, Washington, DC   20036
(202) 797-6000 • fax: (202) 797-6004
e-mail: communications@brookings.edu
website: www.brookings.edu

Founded in 1927, the Brookings Institution conducts research and analyzes global events and their impact on the United States and US foreign policy. It publishes the quarterly *Brookings Review* and numerous books and research papers on foreign policy. Its website publishes editorials, papers, testimony, reports, and articles written by institute scholars, including "Robotic Ethics Won't Clean Up Combat," "Robotic Military Technology Changes Rules of War," and "Unmanned at Any Speed: Bringing Drones into Our National Airspace."

Center for Policy on Emerging Technologies (C-PET)

10 G St. NE, Ste. 710, Washington, DC   20002
(202) 248-5027
e-mail: info@c-pet.org
website: http://c-pet.org

C-PET is a science and technology think tank. The center studies artificial intelligence, robotics, nanotechnologies, biotechnologies, information technologies, and other emerging technologies that have the potential to profoundly affect society. The C-PET Emerging Technologies group is a public listserv that delivers daily news and comments on the latest technological developments. Website visitors can find articles on artificial intelligence and robotics within the Resources link of the website's Network tab, including "Trust Me, I'm a Robot" and "What We Can Learn from Robots."

Center for Strategic and International Studies (CSIS)

1800 K St. NW, Washington, DC   20006

(202) 887-0200 • fax (202) 775-3199
e-mail: webmaster@csis.org
website: http://csis.org

CSIS conducts research and develops policy recommendations on a variety of issues, including defense and security strategies, economic development, energy and climate change, global health, technology, and trade. The center publishes the *Washington Quarterly*, recent articles from which are available on its website. CSIS publishes books, reports, newsletters, and commentaries targeted at decision makers in policy, government, business, and academia. Website visitors can access articles on drones and robotic technology through the website's search engine.

Georgia Institute of Technology, Mobile Robot Laboratory

Technology Square Research Bldg., Rm. S27, 85 Fifth St. NW
Atlanta, GA   30308
(404) 894-2000
e-mail: robot-lab-www@cc.gatech.edu
website: www.cc.gatech.edu/ai/robot-lab

The goal of the Mobile Robot Laboratory is to discover and develop fundamental scientific principles and practices that are applicable to intelligent mobile robot systems. The lab also aims to use its research to solve real-world problems for a wide range of applications. Its publications link provides access to articles on robotic technology, including "The Robot Didn't Do It," "Robots That Need to Mislead: Biologically-Inspired Machine Deception," and "Designing Autonomous Robot Missions with Performance Guarantees."

Humanity+ (formerly The World Transhumanist Association)

5042 Wilshire Blvd., #14334, Los Angeles, CA   90036
(310) 916-9676.
e-mail: info@humanityplus.org
website: http://humanityplus.org

Humanity+ is an international nonprofit membership organization that advocates the ethical use of technology to expand human capacities. The organization supports the development of and access to new technologies that enable people to enjoy better minds, better bodies, and better lives. Humanity+ focuses its activities on how emerging technologies, including robotics, impact the rights of the person, enable people to live longer and better lives, and provide a future-friendly culture. The organization publishes a periodicale called *H+*, which covers technological, scientific, and cultural trends that have the potential to change human beings in fundamental ways. Selected articles from *H+*, including those on robot emotions and robot sex, are available on its website.

The Lifeboat Foundation

1638 Esmeralda Ave., Minden, NV   89423
(775) 329-0180 • fax: (775) 329-0190
e-mail: lifeboat@lifeboat.com
website: http://lifeboat.com

The Lifeboat Foundation is a nonprofit, nongovernmental organization dedicated to encouraging scientific advancements while helping humanity survive existential risks and possible misuse of increasingly powerful technologies, including genetic engineering, nanotechnology, and robotics/AI. The Lifeboat Foundation believes that in some situations it might be feasible to relinquish technological capacity in the public interest. The organization publishes a monthly newsletter called *Lifeboat News*. Links to articles and blogs on androids and artificial intelligence are available on its website.

Machine Intelligence Research Institute (MIRI)

2721 Shattuck Ave., #1023, Berkeley, CA   94705
website: http://intelligence.org

A networking center for scientists, entrepreneurs, and investors involved in emerging technologies, the Machine Intelligence Research Institute (formerly called the Singularity Institute) studies the impact of advanced artificial intelligence on the future. When machines surpass the human ability to design artificial intelligence, they will be able to recursively improve their own intelligence in a way that could quickly lead to an intelligence explosion. Thus, one of MIRI's goals is to ensure that the effects of advanced machine intelligence are beneficial for society. The website research link provides access to blogs, fact sheets, articles, and reports, including "Intelligence Explosion: Evidence and Import," "The Singularity and Machine Ethics," and "Safety Engineering for Artificial General Intelligence."

National Science Foundation (NSF)
4201 Wilson Blvd., Arlington, VA   22230
(703) 292-5111
e-mail: info@nsf.gov
website: www.nsf.gov

The NSF is an independent federal agency created by Congress in 1950 "to promote the progress of science; to advance the national health, prosperity, and welfare; to secure the national defense." The NSF website provides links to foundation "discoveries," which include discoveries in robotic technology. The website's publication search engine also includes articles on robotic technology, robotics education, and robotics initiatives.

Robotics Institute at Carnegie Mellon University
5000 Forbes Ave., Pittsburgh, PA   15213-3890
(412) 268-3818 • fax: (412) 268-6436
website: www.ri.cmu.edu

The Robotics Institute conducts basic and applied research in robotics technologies relevant to industrial and societal tasks. It also collaborates with government, industry, and nonprofit organizations in the areas of sponsored research and education. The institute has spawned over thirty spin-off companies. Website visitors can access its publications in many places, including the authors' home pages and the pages for the lab, group, or project under which the research was conducted. The institute also publishes the *Journal of Field Robotics*; the first issue of each year is available for free online at www.journalfieldrobotics.org/Home.html.

SRI International Artificial Intelligence Center (AIC)

333 Ravenswood Ave., Menlo Park, CA   94025-3493
(650) 859-2641 • fax: (650) 859-3735
e-mail: aic@ai.sri.com
website: www.ai.sri.com

The AIC is a major center for research on artificial intelligence and part of the Stanford Research Institute (SRI), an independent nonprofit research institute that conducts contract research and development for government and business. Founded in 1966, the AIC has been a pioneer in the development of complex computer capabilities. It studies the computational principles underlying intelligence in man and machines with the goal of developing computer-based systems that solve problems, communicate with people, and perceive and interact with the physical world. Many of the AIC's research staff have published books. Articles on robotic technology are also available on its publication search engine.

Bibliography of Books

Yoseph Bar-Cohen, David Hanson, and Adi Marom

The Coming Robot Revolution: Expectations and Fears About Emerging Intelligent, Humanlike Machines. New York: Springer, 2009.

Michael Barnes and Florian Jentsch, eds.

Human-Robot Interactions in Future Military Operations. Burlington, VT: Ashgate, 2010.

Shahzad Bashir and Robert D. Crews, eds.

Under the Drones: Modern Lives in the Afghanistan-Pakistan Borderlands. Cambridge, MA: Harvard University Press, 2012.

Gregory Benford and Elisabeth Malartre

Beyond Human: Living with Robots and Cyborgs. New York: Forge, 2008.

Rodney Brooks

Flesh and Machines: How Robots Will Change Us. New York: Pantheon Books, 2002.

Erik Brynjolfsson and Andrew McAfee

Race Against the Machine: How the Digital Revolution Is Accelerating Innovation, Driving Productivity, and Irreversibly Transforming Employment and the Economy. Lexington, MA: Digital Frontier Press, 2012.

Peter H. Diamandis and Steven Kotler

Abundance: The Future Is Better than You Think. New York: Free Press, 2012.

Martin Ford   *The Lights in the Tunnel: Automation, Accelerating Technology and the Economy of the Future.* United States: Acculant, 2009.

Keith Frankish and William Ramsey, eds.   *Cambridge Handbook of Artificial Intelligence.* Cambridge: Cambridge University Press, 2011.

E.L. Gaston, ed.   *Laws of War and 21st-Century Conflict.* New York: International Debate Education Association, 2012.

J.P. Gunderson and L.F. Gunderson   *Robots, Reasoning, and Reification.* New York: Springer, 2009.

J. Storrs Hall   *Beyond AI: Creating the Conscience of the Machine.* Amherst, NY: Prometheus Books, 2007.

Jeff Hawkins and Sandra Blakeslee   *On Intelligence.* New York: Times Books, 2004.

Armin Krishnan   *Killer Robots: Legality and Ethicality of Autonomous Weapons.* Burlington, VT: Ashgate, 2009.

James Howard Kunstler   *Too Much Magic: Wishful Thinking, Technology, and the Fate of the Nation.* New York: Atlantic Monthly Press, 2012.

Ray Kurzweil   *How to Create a Mind: The Secret of Human Thought Revealed.* New York: Viking, 2012.

Ray Kurzweil — *The Singularity Is Near: When Humans Transcend Biology.* New York: Penguin, 2005.

Roger D. Launius and Howard E. McCurdy — *Robots in Space: Technology, Evolution, and Interplanetary Travel.* Baltimore: Johns Hopkins University Press, 2008.

David N.L. Levy — *Robots Unlimited: Life in a Virtual Age.* Wellesley, MA: A.K. Peters, 2006.

Patrick Lin, Keith Abney, and George A. Bekey, eds. — *Robot Ethics: The Ethical and Social Implications of Robotics.* Cambridge, MA: MIT Press, 2011.

David McFarland — *Guilty Robots, Happy Dogs: The Question of Alien Minds.* New York: Oxford University Press, 2008.

Gaurav S. Sukhatme, ed. — *The Path to Autonomous Robots: Essays in Honor of George A. Bekey.* New York: Springer, 2009.

Jocelyne Troccaz — *Medical Robotics.* Hoboken, NJ: Wiley, 2012.

Kevin Warwick — *Artificial Intelligence: The Basics.* New York: Routledge, 2012.

Index